DOVER · THRIFT · EDITIONS

Book of African-American Quotations

EDITED BY JOSLYN PINE

DOVER PUBLICATIONS, INC.
Mineola, New York

DOVER THRIFT EDITIONS

GENERAL EDITOR: MARY CAROLYN WALDREP
EDITOR OF THIS VOLUME: SUSAN L. RATTINER

DEDICATION

To Mae Julye, my saving grace

Bibliographical Note

Book of African-American Quotations is a new collection of quotations, first published by Dover Publications, Inc., in 2011. Minor style inconsistencies may be due to the practice of preserving the style of each individual quote precisely as it appears in the source.

Library of Congress Cataloging-in-Publication Data

Book of African-American quotations / edited by Joslyn Pine.
    p. cm.—(Dover thrift editions)
Includes bibliographical references.
ISBN-13: 978-0-486-47589-9
ISBN-10: 0-486-47589-1
1. African Americans—Quotations. I. Pine, Joslyn T.
PN6081.3.B66 2011
081'.089'96073—dc22   2010038313

Manufactured in the United States by Courier Corporation
47589103
www.doverpublications.com

Contents

Introduction

The original intention of this collection could be aptly summed up by the words of writer-comedian Bill Cosby in describing his own modus operandi: "I try to keep my humor away from specific 'black' and make it pertain to the general 'human.'" In this case, focusing on African-American wit and wisdom as it pertains to the human condition over racial status. However, as time went on, the book seemed to take on a shape of its own, and what emerged instead is a portrait of another America that went right to the heart of the black experience. Whether the individual was speaking from a time long past, or as recently as last month, no matter what the profession or how high the celebrity on the scale of fame and fortune, everyone had their own singular contribution to make to this pastiche of voices, about how their black heritage had affected their lives, and how they had succeeded despite or because of it—or both.

Why the racial theme is central to the lives of all African Americans is well expressed by the words of John Hope Franklin, writer and historian.

> Racial segregation, discrimination, and degradation are no unanticipated accidents in this nation's history. They stem logically and directly from the legacy that the founding fathers bestowed upon contemporary America. . . . [W]hen the colonists emerged victorious from their war with England, they had both their independence and their slaves.

Just when the colonists had gained their independence from an oppressive foreign regime, the blacks of the young nation would still need to struggle mightily for nearly a century more before they would win *their* freedom. But Lincoln's Emancipation Proclamation was merely one victory along the way, with the greater battles for equal rights yet to be won. In fact, African Americans have had to wait nearly 150 years since slavery's end to see an African-American president, and experienced it as a huge milestone simply because, for most of U.S. history, the idea was unimaginable.

Another theme whose variations play out over and over in the current volume is the fact that for African Americans, art is necessarily political. The individuals will speak for themselves, but it seems appropriate to add here the words of writer W. E. B. Du Bois by way of explanation.

All art is propaganda and ever must be, despite the wailing of the purists. I stand in utter shamelessness and say that whatever art I have for writing has been used always for propaganda for gaining the right of black folk to love and enjoy.

For African Americans, for whom political and cultural visibility has been so hard-won, art has always been a primary means of expression—for being seen or heard—whether in the visual or performing arts or in literature and music. The validity of that statement is probably most manifest in American music, since it grew directly from black roots.

The book's new driving force, as it finally evolved, can best be described by the words of Attorney General Eric Holder, Jr.—that "One cannot truly understand America without understanding the historical experience of black people in this nation. Simply put, to get to the heart of this country one must examine its racial soul."

* * *

The thumbnail biographies are necessarily brief for reasons of space and contain only a fraction of what might otherwise be said about each individual. Hopefully, enough information has been provided to point the way for the interested, curious, or inspired reader to easily pursue any subject. Please note that for every living individual who has a place in this collection, many if not most of the biographical points refer to achievements that span the course of their life and career, and may not refer to current endeavors.

One of the great challenges of compiling a book of quotes is finding worthy material that can stand on its own without an immediate context. That fact, to a great extent, was a guiding principle in the selection of individuals and quotations included. So the process by necessity had to be a purely subjective one. Excerpts from poetry and works of fiction are included, as well as song lyrics; and a quote from such a source may then reflect more indirectly upon its creator.

Since a wide variety of materials were used to compile this collection, spelling and punctuation have, for the most part, been modernized and standardized for the sake of clarity and consistency. Since four different sources might each contain a different version of the same quote, every effort has been made to present the version closest to the spirit and substance of the original. Some were culled from their source in the course of research for this book, and appear here as a quote perhaps for the first time. The parlance of the respective times (which may be offensive to some) remains unchanged for the sake of historical authenticity—and truth.

June 2010   JOSLYN PINE

KEY TO ACRONYMS

CORE = Congress of Racial Equality

NAACP = National Association for the Advancement of Colored
People

NOW = National Organization for Women

SCLC = Southern Christian Leadership Conference

SNCC = Student Nonviolent Coordinating Committee

Hank Aaron

Born 1934 ◆ major league baseball player and executive with the
Atlanta Braves' organization ◆ first MLB player to hit 500 home
runs and reach 3,000 hits ◆ Baseball Hall of Fame
◆ autobiography, *I Had a Hammer*

A white child might need a role model, but a black child needs
more than that in this society. He needs hope.

I never doubted my ability, but when you hear all your life
you're inferior, it makes you wonder if the other guys have something you've never seen before. If they do, I'm still looking
for it.

On the field, blacks have been able to be super giants. But once our
playing days are over, this is the end of it and we go back to the back
of the bus again.

[on breaking Babe Ruth's home run record] I had to break that
record. I had to do it for Jackie [Robinson] and my people and
myself and for everybody who ever called me nigger.

[on retirement] You can only milk a cow so long, and then you're left
holding the pail.

Kareem Abdul-Jabbar

Born 1947 ◆ a.k.a. Ferdinand Lewis "Lew" Alcindor ◆ basketball
player, writer, TV and film actor ◆ winner of six MVP Awards and
six NBA championships ◆ books include *On the Shoulders of
Giants: My Journey Through the Harlem Renaissance,* and an
autobiography, *Giant Steps*

You can't win unless you learn how to lose.

I learned early on that there's a place inside oneself that no one else can violate, that no one else can enter, and that we have a right to protect that place.

I try to do the right thing at the right time. They may just be little things, but usually they make the difference between winning and losing.

Malcolm [X] was talking about real people doing real things, black pride, and Islam. I just grabbed on to it. And I have never looked back.

I'm not comfortable being preachy, but more people have to start spending as much time in the library as they do on the basketball court. If they took the idea that they could escape poverty through education, I think it would make a more basic and long-lasting change in the way things happen.

All the courage and competitiveness of Jackie Robinson affects me to this day. If I patterned my life after anyone, it was him, not because he was the first black baseball player in the majors but because he was a hero.

[*on retirement*] The sport goes on. People will find new heroes. And I'm flattered they'll be compared with me.

African-American Aphorisms

◆ various anonymous sources ◆

We ain't what we ought to be and we ain't what we want to be and we ain't what we're going to be. But thank God we ain't what we was.

Been down so long, down don't worry me.

Blues ain't nothin' but a po' man's heart disease.

All poor people ain't black and all black people ain't poor.

Death don't see no difference 'tween the big house and the cabin.

Don't trouble trouble till trouble troubles you.

Drugs take you further than you want to go, keep you there longer than you want to stay, and cost you more than you can ever pay.

Every shut-eye ain't sleep and every good-bye ain't gone.

Hard work in de hot sun done called a many a man to preach.

Hold a true friend with both hands.

If you ask a Negro where he's been, he'll tell you where he's going.

If you cain't bear no crosses, you cain't wear no crown.

In the South they don't care how close you get, as long as you don't get too high. In the North, they don't care how high you get, as long as you don't get too close.

Life is short and full of blisters.

Mothers raise their daughters and let their sons grow up.

Nothing can suffice a person except that which they have not.

Nothing goes over the devil's back that don't come under his belly.

Old Satan couldn't get along without plenty of help.

Tell the truth and shame the devil.

Romance without finance don't stand a chance.

The higher the monkey climbs, the more he shows his behind.

The man I'll marry ain't born yet—an' his mammy's dead.

The very time I thought I was lost, my dungeon shook and my chains fell off.

The big bee flies high, the little bee makes the honey; the black folks makes the cotton, and the white folks get the money.

The blacker the berry, the sweeter the juice.

Alvin Ailey

1931–1989 ◆ dancer and choreographer who founded the Alvin Ailey American Dance Theater ◆ major works include *Blues Suite* and *Revelations*

The creative process is not controlled by a switch you can simply turn on or off; it's with you all the time.

I am a person who has never completely escaped from the scars of my childhood. Racism, which leaves a shadow on one's sense of accomplishment, can make one feel like a perpetual outsider.

One of the processes of your life is to constantly break down that inferiority, to constantly reaffirm that I Am Somebody.

One of the worst things about racism is what it does to young people.

Jamil Abdullah Al-Amin

Born 1943 ◆ a.k.a. H. Rap Brown ◆ writer and social activist
◆ autobiography, *Die Nigger Die!*

Racism systematically verifies itself anytime the slave can only be free by imitating his master.

I'd rather see a cat with a processed head and a natural mind than a natural head and a processed mind. It ain't what's on your head, it's what's in it.

Being a man is the continuing battle for one's life. One loses a bit of manhood with every stale compromise to the authority of any power in which one does not believe.

Muhammad Ali

Born 1942 ◆ "The Greatest" ◆ world heavyweight championship
boxer and social activist ◆ sports icon ◆ autobiography,
The Greatest: My Own Story

He who is not courageous enough to take risks will accomplish nothing in life.

Champions aren't made in gyms. Champions are made from something they have deep inside them—a desire, a dream, a vision. . . . [T]hey have to have the skill, and the will. But the will must be stronger than the skill.

I hated the sight on TV of big, clumsy, lumbering heavyweights plodding, stalking each other like two Frankenstein monsters, clinging, slugging toe to toe. I knew I could do it better. I would be fast as a lightweight, circle, dance, shuffle, hit, and move . . . dance again and make an art out of it.

The man who views the world at fifty the same way he did at twenty has wasted thirty years of his life.

Float like a butterfly, sting like a bee.

Hating people because of their color is wrong. And it doesn't matter which color does the hating.

I hated every minute of training, but I said, "Don't quit. Suffer now and live the rest of your life as a champion."

It isn't the mountains ahead to climb that wear you out; it's the pebble in your shoe.

Rivers, ponds, lakes and streams—they all have different names, but they all contain water. Just as religions do—they all contain truths.

Only a man who knows what it is like to be defeated can reach down to the bottom of his soul and come up with the extra ounce of power to win when the match is even.

Service to others is the rent you pay for your room here on earth.

Silence is golden when you can't think of a good answer.

The fight is won or lost far away from witnesses—behind the lines, in the gym, and out there on the road, long before I dance under those lights.

Wars of nations are fought to change maps. But wars of poverty are fought to map changes.

Cassius Clay is a slave name. I didn't choose it and I don't want it. I am Muhammad Ali, a free man—it means "Beloved of God"—and I insist that people use it in speaking of and to me.

I am America. I am the part you won't recognize. But get used to me. Black, confident, cocky; my name, not yours; my religion, not yours; my goals, my own; get used to me.

Richard Allen

1760–1831 ✦ minister, educator, writer, and abolitionist ✦ founder
and first bishop of the African Methodist Episcopal (AME) Church

If you love your children, if you love your country, if you love the God of love, clear your hands from slaves, burden not your children or country with them.

We will never separate ourselves voluntarily from the slave population in this country; they are our brethren by the ties of consanguinity, of suffering and of wrong; and we feel there is more virtue in suffering privations with them than fancied advantage for a season.

If you deny us your [Methodist] name, you cannot seal up the Scriptures from us, and deny us a name in heaven.

This land, which we have watered with our tears and our blood, is now our mother country, and we are well satisfied to stay where wisdom abounds and the gospel is free.

Marian Anderson

1897–1993 ◆ opera singer, the first African American to perform at the Metropolitan Opera in a leading role ◆ autobiography, *My Lord, What a Morning*

If you have a purpose in which you can believe, there's no end to the amount of things you can accomplish.

It is easy to look back self-indulgently, feeling pleasantly sorry for oneself and saying I didn't have this and I didn't have that. But it is only the grown woman regretting the hardships of a little girl who never thought they were hardships at all . . . She had the things that really mattered.

Leadership should be born out of the understanding of the needs of those who would be affected by it.

[*on bigotry*] Sometimes, it's like a hair across your cheek. You can't see it, you can't find it with your fingers, but you keep brushing at it because the feel of it is irritating.

Fear is a disease that eats away at logic and makes man inhuman.

Maya Angelou

Born 1928 ◆ writer, poet, playwright, director, producer, educator, dancer, and actress ◆ books include *The Heart of a Woman, Letter to My Daughter*, and *I Know Why the Caged Bird Sings*

I had a heritage, rich and nearer than the tongue which gave it voice. My mind resounded with the words and my blood raced to the rhythms.

At fifteen, life had taught me undeniably that surrender, in its place, was as honorable as resistance, especially if one had no choice.

There is nothing so pitiful as a young cynic because he has gone from knowing nothing to believing nothing.

Without courage we cannot practice any other virtue with consistency.

Life is not measured by the number of breaths we take, but by the moments that take our breath away.

I've learned that making a "living" is not the same thing as making a "life."

I've learned that you shouldn't go through life with a catcher's mitt on both hands; you need to be able to throw something back.

I've learned that even when I have pains, I don't have to be one.

I've learned that people will forget what you said, people will forget what you did, but people will never forget how you made them feel.

Nothing will work unless you do.

There's a world of difference between truth and facts. Facts can obscure truth.

Surviving is important. Thriving is elegant.

Be a rainbow in someone else's cloud.

I believe that the most important single thing, beyond discipline and creativity, is daring to dare.

My mother said I must always be intolerant of ignorance but understanding of illiteracy. That some people, unable to go to school, were more educated and more intelligent than college professors.

History, despite its wrenching pain, cannot be unlived, but if faced with courage, need not be lived again.

The black woman in the South who raises sons, grandsons, and nephews had her heartstrings tied to a hanging noose.

I find it interesting that the meanest life, the poorest existence, is attributed to God's will, but as human beings become more affluent, as their living standard and style begin to ascend the material scale, God descends the scale of responsibility at a commensurate speed.

The needs of society determine its ethics, and in the black American ghettos the hero is that man who is offered only the crumbs from his country's table but by ingenuity and courage is able to take for himself a Lucullan [lavish] feast.

I made the decision to quit show business. Give up the skintight dresses and manicured smiles. The false concern over sentimental lyrics. I would never again work to make people smile inanely and would take on the responsibility of making them think.

Bringing the gifts that my ancestors gave, I am the dream and the hope of the slave. I rise, I rise, I rise.

Louis Armstrong

1901–1971 ◆ "Satchmo" ◆ New Orleans jazz trumpeter, singer, and bandleader ◆ autobiography, *Satchmo: My Life in New Orleans*

We all do "Do, Re, Mi," but you have got to find the other notes yourself.

I didn't wish for anything I couldn't get, and I got pretty near everything I wanted.

The memory of things gone is important to a jazz musician. Things like old folks singing in the moonlight in the back yard on a hot night or something said long ago.

There are some people that if they don't know, you can't tell 'em.

Arthur Ashe

1943–1993 ◆ top-ranking tennis player, writer, and social activist ◆ author of a three-volume history of African-American athletes, *A Hard Road to Glory* ◆ autobiography, *Days of Grace*

Being a black man in America is like having another job.

The black athlete carries the image of the black community. He carries the cross, in a way, until blacks make inroads in other dimensions.

Contemporary black athletes' exploits are well known, but few fully appreciate their true Hard Road to Glory. Discrimination, vilification, incarceration, dissipation, ruination, and ultimate despair have dogged the steps of the mightiest of these heroes.

Sports and politics do mix. Behind the scenes, the two are as inextricably interwoven as any two issues can be. I'm sure politics are involved when teams get franchises or when cities build stadiums. It is unrealistic to say you shouldn't bring politics into sports.

We see basketball players and pop singers as possible role models, when nothing could be further, in most cases, from their capacities. We blacks look for leadership in men and women of such youth and inexperience, as well as poverty of education and character, that it is no wonder that we sometimes seem rudderless.

Racism is not an excuse to not do the best you can.

Pearl Bailey

1918–1990 ◆ actress, singer, and dancer ◆ shows include *St. Louis Woman, House of Flowers*, and *Hello, Dolly!* ◆ films include *Carmen Jones* and *Porgy and Bess* ◆ autobiography, *The Raw Pearl*

We're a great heart people.

There's a period of life when we swallow a knowledge of ourselves and it becomes either good or sour inside.

People see God every day. They just don't recognize Him.

[on audiences] I see their souls, and I hold them in my hands, and because I love them they weigh nothing.

No one can figure out your worth but you.

There is a way to look at the past. Don't hide from it. It will not catch you—if you don't repeat it.

James Baldwin

1924–1987 ◆ novelist, poet, essayist, playwright, and civil rights activist ◆ best-known works include *Go Tell It on the Mountain, The Fire Next Time*, and *Notes of a Native Son*

Children have never been very good at listening to their elders, but they have never failed to imitate them.

Color is not a human or a personal reality; it is a political reality.

They saw themselves as others had seen them. They had been formed by the images made of them by those who had had the deepest necessity to despise them.

It is hard to imitate a people whose existence appears, mainly, to be made tolerable by their bottomless gratitude that they are not, thank heaven, *you.*

Women manage, quite brilliantly, on the whole, and to stunning and unforeseeable effect, to survive and surmount being defined by others. . . . But men are neither so supple nor so subtle. A man fights for his manhood: that's the bottom line.

That marvelously mocking, salty authority with which black men walked was dictated by the tacit and shared realization of the price each had paid to be able to walk at all.

The male cannot bear very much humiliation; and he really cannot bear it, it obliterates him.

The wretched of the earth do not decide to become extinct, they resolve, on the contrary, to multiply: life is their weapon against life, life is all that they have.

Man cannot live by profit alone.

A child cannot be taught by someone who despises him.

The only thing that white people have that black people need, or should want, is power—and no one holds power forever.

Despite the terrorization which the Negro in America endured and endures sporadically . . . despite the cruel and totally inescapable ambivalence of his status in this country, the battle for his identity has long ago been won. He is not a visitor to the West, but a citizen there, an American.

Hatred, which could destroy so much, never failed to destroy the man who hated.

In the context of the Negro problem neither whites nor blacks, for excellent reasons of their own, have the faintest desire to look back; but I think that the past is all that makes the present coherent, and further, that the past will remain horrible for exactly as long as we refuse to assess it honestly.

Money it turned out was exactly like sex; you thought of nothing else if you didn't have it and thought of other things if you did.

To be born in a free society and not be born free is to be born into a lie.

The black man has functioned in the white man's world as a fixed star, as an immovable pillar: and as he moves out of his place, heaven and earth are shaken to their foundations.

I imagine that one of the reasons people cling to their hates so stubbornly is because they sense, once hate is gone, that they will be forced to deal with pain.

To be sensual, I think, is to respect and rejoice in the force of life, of life itself, and to be *present* in all that one does, from the effort of loving to the breaking of bread.

The most dangerous creation of any society is that man who has nothing to lose.

Know whence you came. If you know whence you came, there is really no limit to where you can go.

Benjamin Banneker

1731–1806 ◆ self-educated mathematician, astronomer, inventor, and surveyor ◆ published an annual almanac, 1791–1802 ◆ surveyed the area now known as the District of Columbia in President Washington's time

Presumption should never make us neglect that which appears easy to us, nor despair make us lose courage at the sight of difficulties.

The colour of the skin is in no way connected with strength of the mind or intellectual powers.

[two excerpts from a letter to Thomas Jefferson follow, August 19, 1791]

I freely and cheerfully acknowledge, that I am of the African race, and in the colour which is natural to them of the deepest dye; and it is under a sense of the most profound gratitude to the Supreme Ruler of the Universe, that I now confess to you, that I am not under that tyrannical thralldom, and inhuman captivity to which too many of my brethren are doomed.

[American Revolution vis-à-vis Slavery] Although you were so fully convinced of the benevolence of the Father of Mankind, and of his equal and impartial distribution of these rights and privileges, which he hath conferred upon them, that you should at the same time counteract his mercies, in detaining by fraud and violence so numerous a part of my brethren, under groaning captivity and cruel oppression, that you should at the same time be guilty of that most criminal act, which you professedly detested in others, with respect to yourselves.

Imamu Amiri Baraka

Born 1934 ◆ a.k.a. LeRoi Jones ◆ poet, playwright, and activist
◆ his works include *Blues People: Negro Music in White America*,
and the plays, *Dutchman* and *The Slave*

In America, black *is* a country.

God has been replaced, as he has all over the West, with respectability and air conditioning.

Thought is more important than art. . . . To revere art and have no understanding of the process that forces it into existence, is finally not even to understand what art is.

I took up with the Beats because that's what I saw taking off and flying and somewhat resembling myself. The open and implied rebellion—of form and content. Aesthetic as well as social and political. But I saw most of it as Art.

These have been our White Ages, and all learning has suffered. . . . What the Black Man must do now is look down at the ground upon which he stands, and claim it as his own.

As I stared at the books, I suddenly understood that I didn't know a hell of a lot about anything. What it was that seemed to move me then was that learning was *important*. . . . I vowed, right then, to learn something new every day. It was a deep revelation, something I felt throughout my whole self.

Despair sits on this country in most places like a charm, but there is a special gray death that loiters in the streets.

The Black Artist's role in America is to aid in the destruction of America as he knows it.

Charles Barkley

Born 1963 ◆ "Sir Charles" ◆ basketball player ◆ one of the "Fifty
Greatest Players in NBA History" ◆ winner of two Olympic gold
medals ◆ memoir, *I May Be Wrong but I Doubt It*

If I weren't earning more than $3 million a year to dunk a basketball, most people on the street would run in the other direction if they saw me coming.

Kids are great. That's one of the best things about our business, all the kids you get to meet. It's a shame they have to grow up to be regular people and come to the games and call you names.

I'm not a role model. . . . Just because I dunk a basketball doesn't mean I should raise your kids.

I know I'm never as good or bad as one single performance. I've never believed my critics or my worshippers, and I've always been able to leave the game at the arena.

I love New York City; I've got a gun.

The only difference between a good shot and a bad shot is if it goes in or not.

Poor people cannot rely on the government to come to help you in times of need. You have to get your education. Then nobody can control your destiny.

These are my new shoes. They're good shoes. They won't make you rich like me, they won't make you rebound like me, they definitely won't make you handsome like me. They'll only make you have shoes like me.

Sometimes that light at the end of the tunnel is a train.

Count Basie

1904–1984 ◆ jazz pianist and bandleader ◆ jazz icon ◆ hits
include "One O'Clock Jump," "Jumpin' at the Woodside," and
"April in Paris" ◆ autobiography, *Good Morning Blues*

Of course, there are a lot of ways you can treat the blues, but it will still be the blues.

If you play a tune and a person don't tap their feet, don't play the tune.

[*on the subject of his name*] I knew about King Oliver, and I also knew that Paul Whiteman was called the King of Jazz. Duke Ellington was also getting to be one of the biggest new names in Harlem and also on records and on the radio. And Earl Hines and Baron Lee were also important names. So I decided that I would be one of the biggest new names; and I actually had some little fancy business cards printed up to announce it, COUNT BASIE. Beware the Count is Here.

Life is a bitch, and if it's not one damn thing, it's going to be something else. . . . You don't let that stop you.

Daisy Bates

1914–1999 ♦ civil rights activist, writer, and publisher
♦ accompanied the nine children who desegregated Central H.S.
in Little Rock, Arkansas, in 1957 ♦ founded a newspaper, the
Arkansas State Press ♦ memoir, *The Long Shadow of Little Rock*

[*on Little Rock, 1957*] The crowd moved in closer and then began to follow me, calling me names. I still wasn't afraid. Just a little bit nervous, whether I could make it to the center entrance a block away. It was the longest block I ever walked in my whole life.

We've got to decide if it's going to be this generation or never.

Melba Pattillo Beals

Born 1941 ♦ reporter and educator ♦ member of the Little Rock
Nine who participated in the 1957 desegregation of Central H.S.
♦ memoir, *Warriors Don't Cry*

The first day I approached Central H.S., my heart pounded in my ears. My face was hot; I was so frightened about what would happen to me. . . . My skin was stinging. I was right, because the very first day I was chased away by men carrying ropes, men from the white segregationist mob who threatened to kill me.

When I entered the school protected by the 101st Airborne soldiers, sent by the President to enforce the law and hold off the segregationist mob, I felt proud to be an American. . . . I thought to myself, if they just get to know me, if they understand that I'm smart, I'm clean, that I wear nice clothes, that I polish my saddle shoes, and I sing, they will understand that although my color is brown, I am no different than they are.

My grandmother India—who had been a maid—thought that my integrating Central was a way of assuring that I wouldn't be a maid too. It was a way of demanding that I would be treated equally and have equal opportunity, a life that she never had.

If someone called me names or spat on me, or kicked me in the shin, or walked on my heel, I thought I couldn't make it one more moment. But each time I would go home, and my grandmother would point out that what I was doing was not for myself, but for generations yet unborn.

We have made progress. . . . It is a long, long way from being a little girl who grew up in Little Rock and sat in the back of the bus, and drank from water fountains marked colored, and went to a black school in an apartheid society.

Romare Bearden

1911–1988 ✦ experimental artist and writer ✦ helped create a jazz aesthetic in visual art ✦ the Museum of Modern Art in NYC honored him with a one-man show in 1970

There are roads out of the secret places within us along which we all must move as we go to touch others.

I do not need to go looking for "happenings," the absurd, or the surreal because I have seen things that neither Dalí, Beckett, Ionesco, nor any of the others could have thought possible; and to see these things I did not need to do more than look out of my studio window.

I am a man concerned with truth, not flattery, who shares a dual culture that is unwilling to deny the Harlem where I grew up or the Haarlem of the Dutch masters that contributed its element to my understanding of art.

[about his style] Well, it's like jazz; you do this and then you improvise.

I create social identities so far as the subjects are Negro. But I have not created protest images, because the world within the collage, if it is authentic, retains the right to speak for itself.

Derrick Bell

Born 1930 ◆ legal scholar, writer, educator, and civil rights activist
◆ works include *Faces at the Bottom of the Well: The Permanence
of Racism* and *And We Are Not Saved: The Elusive Quest
for Racial Justice*

Black people are the magical faces at the bottom of society's well. Even the poorest whites, those who must live their lives only a few levels above, gain their self-esteem by gazing down on us. Surely, they must know that their deliverance depends on letting down their ropes.

We yearn that our civil rights work will be crowned with success, but what we really want—want even more than success—is meaning.

It appears that my worst fears have been realized: we have made progress in everything yet nothing has changed.

Lerone Bennett, Jr.

Born 1928 ◆ journalist, educator, and social historian ◆ books
include *Before the Mayflower: A History of Black America* and
Forced into Glory: Abraham Lincoln's White Dream

History says we can and will survive if we do what our spiritual tells us: "Keep your hand on the plow, hold on."

Violence always rebounds, always returns home.

History tells us a nation can survive for years by shifting the burdens of life to the people confined by force and violence to the bottom.

It is not true, as so many commentators have said, that Nat Turner initiated a wave of violence in Southampton [County, VA]. The violence was already there. Slavery was violence.

An educator in a system of oppression is either a revolutionary or an oppressor.

We misunderstand racism completely if we do not understand that racism is a mask for a much deeper problem involving not the victims of racism but the perpetrators.

Chuck Berry

Born 1926 ◆ "Father of Rock 'n' Roll" ◆ singer-songwriter ◆ hits
include such classics as "Johnny B. Goode," "Maybellene," and
"Sweet Little Sixteen" ◆ autobiography, *Chuck Berry*

Don't let the same dog bite you twice.

The only Maybellene I knew was the name of a cow.

Roll over, Beethoven, and tell Tchaikovsky the news.

Mother and Daddy were of the Baptist faith and sang in the Antioch
Church choir. The choir rehearsed in our home around the upright
piano in the front room. My very first memories, while still in my
baby crib, are of musical sounds.

Rock's so good to me. Rock is my child and my grandfather.

Mary McLeod Bethune

1875–1955 ◆ American educator, feminist, and civil rights leader
◆ founder of the National Council for Negro Women ◆ director
for Negro affairs of the National Youth Administration under
President Franklin D. Roosevelt

Next to God we are indebted to women, first for life itself, and then
for making it worth living.

Cease to be a drudge, seek to be an artist.

Faith is the first factor in a life devoted to service. Without it,
nothing is possible. With it, nothing is impossible.

"Love thy neighbor" is a precept which could transform the world if
it were universally practiced.

I am my mother's daughter, and the drums of Africa still beat in my
heart. They will not let me rest while there is a single Negro boy or
girl without a chance to prove his worth.

There is a place in God's sun for the youth "farthest down" who has
the vision, the determination, and the courage to reach it.

What does the Negro want? His answer is very simple. He wants
only what all other Americans want. He wants opportunity to make
real what the Declaration of Independence and the Constitution
and the Bill of Rights say.

Eubie Blake

1883–1983 ◆ jazz pianist and composer, ragtime artist, and
vaudeville performer (with Noble Sissle, "The Dixie Duo")
◆ Broadway hits include *Shuffle Along, The Chocolate Dandies,*
and *Blackbirds of 1930*

I don't have any bad habits. They might be bad habits for other
people, but they're all right for me.

Be grateful for luck. Pay the thunder no mind—listen to the birds.
And don't hate nobody.

If I'd known I was going to live this long, I'd have taken better care
of myself.

Julian Bond

Born 1940 ◆ writer, educator, social activist, and politician ◆ one
of the founders of SNCC ◆ first president of the Southern Poverty
Law Center and a chairman of the NAACP ◆ books include
Gonna Sit at the Welcome Table and *Eyes on the Prize: America's
Civil Rights Years, 1954–1965*

Violence is black children going to school for twelve years and
receiving six years' worth of education.

As legal slavery passed, we entered into a permanent period of
unemployment and underemployment from which we have yet to
emerge.

The system conceded to black people the right to sit up in the front
of the bus—a hollow victory when one's longest trip is likely to be
from the feudal South to the mechanized poverty of the North.

Many are attracted to social service—the rewards are immediate, the
gratification quick. But if we have social justice, we won't need
social service.

Cory A. Booker

Born 1969 ◆ community activist, scholar, attorney, and
All-American football player ◆ mayor of Newark, New Jersey since
2006 ◆ on April 2, 2010, Newark celebrated its first homicide-free
month in forty years

We're Brick City [Newark] because we're tough, we're resilient, we're strong, we're enduring and, most important, when we come together there's nothing we can't create.

If you wanna earn, baby, earn, you gotta learn, baby, learn!

Arna Bontemps

1902–1973 ◆ poet, writer, historian, librarian, and editor ◆ Harlem
Renaissance notable ◆ his first novel, *God Sends Sunday*, was
adapted into the play, *St. Louis Woman* ◆ other works include
Black Thunder and a children's book, *The Story of the Negro*

You don't want to stand on a corner and be told to get off it when you got nowhere else to go. And we want somewhere else to go.

Is there something we have forgotten? Some precious thing we have lost, wandering in strange lands?

If there can be returning after death, I shall come back. But it will not be here; if you want me you must search for me beneath the palms of Africa.

Let us keep the dance of rain our fathers kept, and tread our dreams beneath the jungle sky.

Donna Brazile

Born 1959 ◆ community activist, campaign manager, and educator
◆ memoir, *Cooking with Grease: Stirring the Pots in America*
◆ the first African-American woman to lead a presidential
campaign ("Gore for President")

Civic education and civic responsibility should be taught in elementary school.

The role of a community organizer is to help people in distress.

If you're not out front defining your vision, your opponent will spend gobs of money to define it for you.

We're like a Third World country when it comes to some of our election practices.

The 2000 election exposed some ugly history in our country.

Lou Brock

Born 1939 ◆ major league baseball player and special instructor coach ◆ Baseball Hall of Fame ◆ recipient of the Babe Ruth Award ◆ memoir, *Stealing Is My Game*

[When] Jim Crow was king . . . I heard a game in which Jackie Robinson was playing, and I felt pride in being alive. The baseball field was my fantasy of what life offered.

You can't be afraid to make errors! You can't be afraid to be naked before the crowd, because no one can ever master the game of baseball, or conquer it. You can only challenge it.

Show me a guy who is afraid to look bad, and I'll show you a guy you can beat every time.

Nathaniel H. Bronner, Sr.

1914–1993 ◆ entrepreneur and humanitarian ◆ founded Bronner Bros., one of the largest enterprises specializing in African-American hair and skin care products

Success is when your cup runneth over and your saucer too.

[What follows are some of the principles taught by Dr. Nathaniel H. Bronner, Sr. to his six sons]

Keep God 1st, Family 2nd, and Business 3rd.

Success occurs when preparation meets opportunity.

You only get one body and a man will give all his money to regain his health, so preserve your health.

Learn to grab peace and rest whenever you can; never stand up if you can sit down and never sit down if you can lay down.

Whenever your outgo exceeds your income, then your upkeep will become your downfall.

Your judgment is no better than your information.

You can't fly with eagles if you hang out with turkeys.

Gwendolyn Brooks

1917–2000 ♦ poet, novelist, and educator ♦ first African-American recipient of a Pulitzer Prize for Poetry ♦ poetry consultant for the Library of Congress and poet laureate of Illinois

Art hurts. Art urges voyages—and it is easier to stay at home.

Truth-tellers are not always palatable. There is a preference for candy bars.

The forties and fifties were years of high poet-incense; the language-flowers were thickly sweet. Those flowers whined and begged white folks to pick them, to find them lovable. Then—the sixties: Independent fire!

When I was a child, it did not occur to me, even once, that the black in which I was encased (I called it brown in those days) would be considered, one day, beautiful.

I—who have "gone the gamut" from an almost angry rejection of my dark skin by some of my brainwashed brothers and sisters to a surprised queenhood in the new Black sun—am qualified to enter at least the kindergarten of new consciousness now.

To be in love is to touch things with a lighter hand.

What else is there to say but everything?

Claude Brown

1937–2002 ♦ writer, playwright, and social activist ♦ autobiography and best-known work, *Manchild in the Promised Land*

Every night when Dad went to bed, he'd put his watch, his money, his wallet, and his knife under his pillow. . . . When he got up, he would wind his watch, but he would take more time with his knife. . . . Sometimes he would oil it. He never went out without his knife.

I suppose that regardless of what any Negro in America might do or how high he might rise in social status, he still has something in common with every other Negro.

The children of . . . disillusioned colored pioneers inherited the total lot of their parents—the disappointments, the anger. To add to their misery, they had little hope of deliverance. For where does one run to when he's already in the promised land?

James Brown

1933–2006 ◆ "Godfather of Soul" ◆ singer-songwriter, dancer, bandleader, and record producer ◆ autobiography, *James Brown: The Godfather of Soul*

Say it loud, I'm black and I'm proud!

You can't accomplish anything by blowing up, burning up, stealing, and looting. Don't terrorize. Organize. Don't burn. Give kids a chance to learn . . . The real answer to race problems in this country is education. Not burning and killing. Be ready. Be qualified. Own something. Be somebody. That's Black Power.

My father, with only a second-grade education, was the hardest working man I ever knew. I think I got most of my drive from him.

Sometimes you struggle so hard to feed your family one way, you forget to feed them the other way, with spiritual nourishment. Everybody needs that.

I've been in slavery all my life. Ain't nothing changed for me but the address.

[*on being the "Godfather of Soul"*] I taught them everything they know, but not everything I know.

When I'm on stage, I'm trying to do one thing: bring people joy. Just like church does. People don't go to church to find trouble, they go there to lose it.

It doesn't matter how you travel it, it's the same road. It doesn't get any easier when you get bigger, it gets harder. And it will kill you if you let it.

Les Brown

Born 1945 ◆ writer and motivational speaker ◆ books include
Long Life and Good Days and *Live Your Dreams*

I can't lecture on something unless I am living it.

Mission: [To] help people become uncomfortable with their mediocrity.

No one rises to low expectations.

Too many people interpret success as sainthood. Success does not make you a great person; how you deal with it decides that.

When life knocks you down, try to fall on your back because if you can look up, you can get up.

Ron H. Brown

1941–1996 ◆ attorney, lobbyist, campaign manager, and commerce
secretary (Clinton Administration) ◆ the first African American to
head a political party (Democratic National Committee)

[on the sixties] People were going to bed Negro and waking up black. There were major psychological changes going on.

Every new idea is an impossibility until it is born.

William Wells Brown

c. 1814–1884 ◆ writer, playwright, abolitionist, orator, and historian
◆ works include the novel, *Clotel, or, The President's Daughter:
A Narrative of Slave Life in the United States* and *The Escape, or
A Leap for Freedom*, the first dramatic play by an African American

Behold the Mayflower anchored at Plymouth Rock, the slave ship in the James River. Each a parent, one of the prosperous, labor-honoring, law-sustaining institutions of the North; the other the mother of slavery, idleness, lynch-law, ignorance, unpaid labor, poverty, and ducling, despotism, the ceaseless swing of the whip; and the peculiar institutions of the South.

All I demand for the black man is, that the white people shall take their heels off his neck, and let him have a chance to rise by his own efforts.

This was a Southern auction, at which the bones, muscles, sinews, blood, and nerves of a young lady of sixteen were sold for five hundred dollars; her moral character for two hundred; her improved intellect for one hundred; her Christianity for three hundred; and her chastity and virtue for four hundred dollars more. And this, too, in a city thronged with churches, whose tall spires look like so many signals pointing to heaven, and whose ministers preach that slavery is a God-ordained institution!

Despotism increases in severity with the number of despots; the responsibility is more divided, and the claims more numerous.

No country has produced so much heroism in so short a time, connected with escapes from peril and oppression, as has occurred in the United States among fugitive slaves.

Sad to say, Jefferson is not the only American statesman who has spoken high-sounding words in favour of freedom, and then left his own children to die slaves.

Society does not frown upon the man who sits with his mulatto child upon his knee, whilst its mother stands a slave behind his chair.

The prejudice that exists in the Free States against coloured persons, on account of their colour, is attributable solely to the influence of slavery, and is but another form of slavery itself.

Were I about to tell you the evils of Slavery, to represent to you the Slave in his lowest degradation, I should wish to take you, one at a time, and whisper it to you. Slavery has never been represented. Slavery never can be represented.

Ralph J. Bunche

1904–1971 ◆ statesman, diplomat, educator, and scholar ◆ held
the position of undersecretary-general, the highest-ranking U.S.
official at the United Nations ◆ first African American to win
the Nobel Peace Prize

We must adhere staunchly to the basic principle that anything less than full equality is not enough. If we compromise on that principle, our soul is dead.

We must fight as a race for everything that makes for a better country and a better world. We are dreaming idiots and trusting fools to do anything less.

Hearts are the strongest when they beat in response to noble ideals.

There are no warlike people—just warlike leaders.

Nannie Burroughs

1879–1961 ◆ educator, orator, feminist, and religious leader
◆ helped establish the National Association of Colored Women
◆ founder of the National Training School for Women and Girls

The Negro woman carries the moral destiny of two races in her hand. Had she not been the woman of unusual moral stamina that she is, the black race would have been made a great deal whiter, and the white race a great deal blacker.

It will profit the Negro nothing to enter into an ungodly competition for material possessions when he has gifts of greater value. The most valuable contribution which he can make to American civilization must be made out of his spiritual endowment.

Anything that is as old as racism is in the blood line of the nation. It's not any superficial thing—that attitude is in the blood and we have to educate it out.

Bebe Moore Campbell

1950–2006 ◆ educator, writer, and radio and TV commentator
◆ works include the novel, *Your Blues Ain't Like Mine*, and the children's book, *Sometimes My Mommy Gets Angry* ◆ memoir, *Sweet Summer: Growing Up With and Without My Dad*

[Emmett Till] was a very real ghostlike presence in my life and in the lives of a lot of blacks. He catapulted us into civil rights. He died, he was murdered in August [1955], and [the following December] Rosa Parks refused to move on the bus in Birmingham.

[about her writing] I wanted to give racism a face. African Americans know about racism, but I don't think we really know the causes. I decided it's first of all a family problem.

We've got to start getting past stereotypes, and anger, and fear, if we're going to have any semblance of racial harmony in this country. We have to make color our joy, not our burden.

Geoffrey Canada

Born 1952 ◆ educator, social activist, and writer ◆ president and CEO of the Harlem Children's Zone ◆ author of *Reaching Up for Manhood: Transforming the Lives of Boys in America* and his memoir, *Fish Stick Knife Gun: A Personal History of Violence in America*

[My family was] too poor to dress properly. I had thin socks, thin pants, no sweaters and no boots. It wasn't until years later that I found out you could remain warm in the winter if you had the right clothes.

The greatest risk of being a poor black boy in the ghetto was that you would be robbed of the most sacred thing that you had, your manhood.

The real problem is not single women, it's men who walk away from their families and leave them without support emotionally and financially.

I try to build within each [student] . . . a reservoir of strength that they can draw from as they face the countless tribulations small and large that poor children face every day. And I try to convince each one that I know their true value, their worth as human beings, their special gift that God gave to them.

There may be some in this country who think being poor is a matter of lack of values and determination. But I know it to be something different. You can work hard all your life, have impeccable values and still be poor.

We are in a state of war in the inner cities. I call it America's secret war against itself . . . and the war's chief victims are children.

I want to be a children's hero. Children need heroes because heroes give hope; without hope they have no future.

Stokely Carmichael

1941–1998 ◆ a.k.a. Kwame Ture ◆ civil rights activist ◆ leader of
SNCC and honorary prime minister of the Black Panther Party
◆ autobiography, *Ready for Revolution: The Life and Struggles of
Stokely Carmichael*

We been saying freedom for six years and we ain't got nothin'. What
we gonna start saying now is "Black Power"!

Politically, black power means . . . the coming-together of black
people to elect representatives and *to force those representatives to
speak to their needs.* It does not mean merely putting black faces into
office.

For decades, black people had been taught to believe that voting,
politics, is "white folks' business." And the white folks had indeed
monopolized that business, by methods which ran the gamut from
economic intimidation to murder.

The act of registering to vote . . . gives one a sense of being. The
black man who goes to register is saying to the white man, "No."

The draft exemplifies as much as racism the totalitarianism which
prevails in this nation in the disguise of consensus democracy. The
president has conducted war in Vietnam without the consent of
Congress or the American people, without the consent of anybody
except maybe Lady Bird.

For racism to die, a totally different American must be born.

I'm for the Negro. I'm not anti anything.

Our grandfathers had to run, run, run. My generation's out of
breath. We ain't running no more.

Betty Carter

1929–1998 ◆ jazz and scat singer ◆ started her own label, Bet-Car,
and the Jazz Ahead program for aspiring musicians ◆ paired with
Ray Charles for the instant classic, *Baby, It's Cold Outside*

If you wanted to get into jazz, you had to go downtown where the
pimps, prostitutes, hustlers, gangsters and gamblers supported the

music. If it wasn't for them there would be no jazz! They supported the club-owners who bought the music. It wasn't the middle-class people who said "Let's go hear Charlie Parker tonight."

Billie Holiday was a stylist with a particular and unique sound of her own. She was untrained, unabashed, and uninhibited.

If you're sitting in that audience ready to fight me from the very beginning, I'm going to have a hard time getting to you. But if you've got a heart at all, I'm going to get it.

George Washington Carver

c. 1864–1943 ◆ "Wizard of Tuskegee" ◆ scientist, botanist, educator and inventor ◆ extracted 300 different products from the peanut plant

I love to think of nature as an unlimited broadcasting system, through which God speaks to us every hour, if we will only tune in.

When our thoughts—which bring actions—are filled with hate against anyone, Negro or white, we are in a living hell. That is as real as hell will ever be.

When I was a child, my owner saw what he considered to be a good business deal and immediately accepted it. He traded me off for a horse.

How far you go in life depends on your being tender with the young, compassionate with the aged, sympathetic with the striving, and tolerant of the weak and strong. Because someday in life you will have been all of these.

No individual has any right to come into the world and go out of it without leaving behind him distinct and legitimate reasons for having passed through it.

Most people search high and wide for the keys to success. If they only knew, the key to their dreams lies within.

I wanted to know the name of every stone and flower and insect and beast. I wanted to know where it got its color, where it got its life—but there was no one to tell me.

Fear of something is at the root of hate for others and hate within will eventually destroy the hater.

We have become ninety-nine percent money mad. The method of living at home modestly and within our income, laying a little by systematically for the proverbial rainy day which is due to come, can almost be listed among the lost arts.

Wilt Chamberlain

1936–1999 ◆ "Big Dipper" ◆ basketball player ◆ first player in NBA history named MVP and Rookie of the Year in the same season ◆ autobiography, A *View from Above*

Everybody pulls for David, nobody roots for Goliath.

With all of you men out there who think that having a thousand different ladies is pretty cool, I have learned in my life, I've found out, that having one woman a thousand different times is much more satisfying.

I believe that good things come to those who work.

Ray Charles

1930–2004 ◆ singer, songwriter, arranger, pianist, and soul music pioneer ◆ one of the original inductees into the Rock and Roll Hall of Fame ◆ hits include "I Can't Stop Loving You" and "Georgia on My Mind" ◆ autobiography, *Brother Ray: Ray Charles' Own Story*

I don't sing a song unless I feel it. The song don't tug at my heart, I pass on it. I have to believe in what I'm doing.

I am not a blues singer. I am not a jazz singer. I am not a country singer. But I am a singer who can sing the blues, who can sing jazz, who can sing country.

I was born with music inside me. . . . Music was one of my parts. Like my ribs, my liver, my kidneys, my heart. Like my blood.

Soul [music] is like electricity—we don't know what it is, but it's a force that can light a room.

Going blind. Sounds like a fate worse than death, doesn't it? Seems like something which would get a little kid down, make him afraid, and leave him half-crazy and sad. Well, I'm here to tell you that it didn't happen that way—at least not with me.

I couldn't see the people looking back at me. So I just tried to please myself. I figured if I could please Ray, that was good enough.

Traveling round the world opened up my ears.

Affluence separates people. Poverty knits 'em together. You got some sugar and I don't; I borrow some of yours. Next month you might not have any flour; well, I'll give you some of mine.

I never learned to stop at the skin. If I looked at a man or woman, I wanted to see inside. Being distracted by shading or coloring is stupid. It gets in the way. It's something I just can't see.

My music had roots which I'd dug up from my own childhood, musical roots buried in the darkest soil.

Soul is a way of life, but it is always the hard way.

Charles W. Chesnutt

1858–1932 ◆ short-story writer, novelist, and lecturer ◆ literary
icon who garnered a national reading audience and critical
acclaim, and paved the way for the Harlem Renaissance
writers ◆ books include *The Conjure Woman* and
The Marrow of Tradition

[*on being African American*] It never occurred to me to claim any merit because of it, and I have always resented the denial of anything because of it.

A colored man might be as good as a white man in theory, but neither of them [is] of any special consequence without money, or talent, or position.

As a man sows, so shall he reap. In works of fiction, such men are sometimes converted. More often, in real life, they do not change their natures until they are converted into dust. One does well to distrust a tamed tiger.

Impossibilities are merely things of which we have not yet learned, or which we do not wish to happen.

Our boasted civilization is but a veneer which cracks and scrubs off at the first impact of primal passions.

Race prejudice is the devil unchained.

Selfishness is the most constant of human motives. Patriotism, humanity, or the love of God may lead to sporadic outbursts which sweep away the heaped-up wrongs of centuries; but they languish at times, while the love of self works on ceaselessly, unwearingly, burrowing always at the very roots of life, and heaping up fresh wrongs for other centuries to sweep away.

Sins, like chickens, come home to roost.

Surely, God had put his curse not alone upon the slave, but upon the stealer of men! . . . The weed had been cut down, but its root remained, deeply imbedded in the soil, to spring up and trouble a new generation.

The washtub [is] that last refuge of honest able-bodied poverty, in all countries where the use of clothing is conventional.

The workings of the human heart are the profoundest mystery of the universe. One moment they make us despair of our kind, and the next, we see in them the reflection of the divine image.

Those who set in motion the forces of evil cannot always control them afterwards.

When the pride of intellect and caste is broken; when we grovel in the dust of humiliation; when sickness and sorrow come, and the shadow of death falls upon us, and there is no hope elsewhere—we turn to God, who sometimes swallows the insult, and answers the appeal.

We are all puppets in the hands of Fate, and seldom see the strings that move us.

There's time enough, but none to spare.

Alice Childress

1916–1994 ◆ writer, playwright, actress, director, and lecturer
◆ plays include *Florence* and *Trouble in Mind*, which won an Obie Award ◆ books include *A Hero Ain't Nothin' but a Sandwich* and *Like One of the Family: Conversations from a Domestic's Life*

The black writer explains pain to those who inflict it.

Writers are encouraged to "keep 'em laughing" and complain "with good humor" in order to "win" allies. The joke is always on ourselves.

Like snowflakes, the human pattern is never cast twice. We are uncommonly and marvelously intricate in thought and action, our problems are most complex and, too often, silently borne.

Life is just a short walk from the cradle to the grave—and it sure behooves us to be kind to one another along the way.

I believe racism has killed more people than speed, heroin, or cancer, and will continue to kill until it is no more.

I continue to create because writing is a labor of love and also an act of defiance, a way to light a candle in a gale wind.

Shirley Chisholm .

1924–2005 ◆ educator, politician, civil rights activist, and feminist
◆ the first African-American woman elected to Congress
◆ co-founder of the National Women's Political Caucus
◆ memoir, *Unbought and Unbossed*

It grew on me that we, black men especially, were expected to be subservient even in groups where ostensibly everyone was equal.

Black women are not here to compete or fight with you, brothers. If we have hang-ups about being male or female, we're not going to be able to use our talents to liberate all of our black people.

Racism is so universal in this country, so widespread, and deep-seated, that it is invisible because it is so normal.

Tremendous amounts of talent are lost to our society just because that talent wears a skirt.

When morality comes up against profit, it is seldom that profit loses.

I don't measure America by its achievement, but by its potential.

Black people have freed themselves from the dead weight of the albatross of blackness that once hung around their neck. They have done it by picking it up in their arms and holding it out with pride for all the world to see. They have done it by embracing it—not in the dark of the moon but in the searing light of the white sun. They have said *Yes* to it and found that the skin that was once seen as symbolizing their shame is in reality their badge of honor.

Our children, our jobless men, our deprived, rejected, and starving fellow citizens must come first. For this reason, I intend to vote *No* on every money bill that comes to the floor of this House that provides any funds for the Department of Defense.

I am, as is obvious, both black and a woman. And that is a good vantage point from which to view at least two elements of what is becoming a social revolution: the American black revolution and the women's liberation movement. But it is also a horrible disadvantage. It is a disadvantage because America as a nation is both racist and antifeminist.

Of my two "handicaps," being female put many more obstacles in my path than being black.

John Henrik Clarke

1915–1998 ◆ writer, educator, and historian ◆ pioneer in the field of African-American studies ◆ books include *My Life in Search of Africa* and *Malcolm X: The Man and His Times*

History is a clock that people use to tell the cultural and political time of day. It is also a compass that people use to find themselves on the map of human geography.

Until quite recently, it was rather generally assumed, even among well-educated persons in the West, that the African continent was a great expanse of land, mostly jungle, inhabited by savages and fierce beasts. It was not thought of as an area where great civilizations could have existed.

It's time for black people to stop playing the separating game of geography, of where the slave ship put us down. We must concentrate on where the slave ship picked us up.

In Africa one day, while sitting with some Africans, I saw a white person and I was so secure. For the first time in my life I felt no fear and knew exactly why. I was in a sea of security. There was nothing—absolutely nothing he could do to me.

Ultimately, a sharing society [needs] to come into being to have any society at all, because capitalism is without humanity, without heart, and without concern for people.

We need a revolution inside of our own minds.

Eldridge Cleaver

1935–1998 ◆ radical intellectual, social activist, and writer ◆
best-known work, *Soul on Ice* ◆ minister of information for the
Black Panther Party, and editor of their official newspaper

History could pass for a scarlet text, its jot and tittle graven red in human blood.

Respect commands itself and it can neither be given nor withheld when it is due.

The enemies of black people have learned something from history and they're discovering new ways to divide us faster than we are discovering new ways to unite.

The price of hating other human beings is loving oneself less.

The sins of the fathers are visited upon the heads of the children— but only if the children continue in the evil deeds of the fathers.

Too much agreement kills a chat.

You're either part of the solution or part of the problem.

You don't have to teach people to be human. You have to teach them how to stop being inhuman.

Lucille Clifton

1936–2010 ◆ poet, writer, and educator ◆ poet laureate of
Maryland ◆ winner of a National Book Award ◆ also notable for
books of prose and verse for children that focus on the
African-American experience

I have always known that being very poor, which we were, had nothing to do with lovingness or familyness or character or any of that. . . . We were quite clear that what we had didn't have anything to do with what we were.

Other people think they know how long life is. How strong life is. We know.

[on slavery] Even the good part was awful.

Sometimes I think that the most anger comes from ones who were late in discovering that when the world said nigger it meant them too.

We have a generation enslaving itself to drugs, young men and women doing to our race what slavery couldn't.

When a man walk manly he don't stumble even in the lion's den.

Johnnie Cochran

1937–2005 ♦ lawyer best known for his leadership role in the O. J. Simpson case, "The Trial of the Century" ♦ other high-profile clients included Sean Combs, Michael Jackson, and Rosa Parks ♦ memoir, A *Lawyer's Life*

We've got to be judged by how we do in times of crisis.

[The] issue of police abuse really galvanized the minority community. It taught me that these cases could really get attention.

I have learned not to be thin-skinned, especially when I think I'm doing the right thing. It's not about money, it's about using the law as a device for change.

Money will determine whether the accused goes to prison or walks out of the courtroom a free man.

If it doesn't fit, you must acquit.

Johnnetta B. Cole

Born 1936 ♦ educator, anthropologist, and feminist ♦ first African-American woman president of Spelman College, Atlanta ♦ books include *Gender Talk. The Struggle for Women's Equality in African-American Communities*

If folk can learn to be racist, then they can learn to be antiracist. If being a sexist ain't genetic, then, dad gum, people can learn about gender equality.

In the long run . . . the real horror of oppression is that it can rob people of their will to try, and make them take themselves out of the running of life.

Making do when DON'T prevails is, quite simply, a kind of genius.

The histories of the poor and the powerless are as important as those of their conquerors, their colonizers, their kings and queens.

The first sign of an educated person is that she asks more questions than she delivers answers.

I need to keep thinking and analyzing, and have that transformed onto a piece of paper. Besides, if we as African-American women don't write our own books, then other folks will continue to define us.

Never acquire a lifestyle you're willing to sell your soul to keep.

While it is true that without a vision the people perish, it is doubly true that without action the people and their vision perish as well.

The legacy of courage left by heroic black women was amassed, deed by deed, day by day, without praise or encouragement.

The more we pull together toward a new day, the less it matters what pushed us apart in the past.

Nat "King" Cole

1919–1965 ◆ Singer, song stylist, pianist, actor, TV personality, and recording artist ◆ first came to prominence as a jazz pianist and vocalist with the King Cole Trio ◆ hit songs include "Mona Lisa," "Unforgettable," and "Too Young"

Sponsors don't have guts. Madison Avenue is afraid of the dark.

I can't come in on a one-night stand and overpower the law. The whites come to applaud a Negro performer like the colored do. When you've got the respect of white and colored, you can ease a lot of things . . . I can help ease the tension by gaining the respect of both races all over the country.

The people who know nothing about music are the ones always talking about it.

Mine is a casual approach to a song; I lean heavily on the lyrics. By that I mean I try to tell a story with the melody as background.

I make no claim to being a business genius. You can make so much money in this business that it loses its value.

I'm not playing for other musicians. We're trying to reach the guy who works all day and wants to spend a buck at night. We'll keep him happy.

Ornette Coleman

Born 1930 ◆ innovative alto sax player, composer, and improviser
◆ compositions include jazz and modern classical pieces ◆
created the jazz-rock fusion genre he dubbed "harmolodic"

I'm interested in music, not in my image. If someone plays something fantastic, that I could never have thought of, it makes me happy to know it exists. Only America makes you feel that everybody wants to be like you. That's what success is: Everybody wants to be like you.

I sometimes realize that there is something on the earth that is free of everything but what created it, and that is the one thing I have been trying to find.

Jazz is the only music in which the same note can be played night after night but differently each time.

Marva Collins

Born 1936 ◆ educator and author ◆ established her own school,
the Westside Preparatory School, in Chicago ◆ her book,
Marva Collins' Way, is about her innovative teaching methods

Excellence is not an act but a habit. The things you do the most are the things you do the best.

Character is what you know you are, not what others think you have.

I have proven that children labeled "untouchable" can learn.

[of her students] None of you has ever failed. School may have failed you.

John Coltrane

1926–1967 ◆ sax player, composer, and recording artist ◆ icon of
modern jazz ◆ some of his compositions were created
spontaneously as they were played onstage ◆ albums include
My Favorite Things and *A Love Supreme*

I have to feel that I'm after something. If I make money, fine. But I'd rather be striving. It's the striving, man, it's that I want.

[God] is gracious and merciful. His way is through love in which we all are. It is truly—a Love SUPREME.

I think music can make the world better and, if I'm qualified, I want to do it. I'd like to point out to people the divine in a musical language that transcends words. I want to speak to their souls.

By this point I don't know what else can be said in words about what I'm doing. Let the music speak for itself.

Anna Julia Cooper

1858–1964 ◆ educator, scholar, and activist in the women's and
Pan-African movements ◆ best-known book is *A Voice from
the South*, a landmark feminist text

Only the black woman can say "when and where I enter, in the quiet, undisputed dignity of my womanhood, without violence and without suing or special patronage, then and there the whole Negro race enters with me."

I constantly felt (as I suppose many an ambitious girl has felt) a thumping from within unanswered by any beckoning from without.

The cause of freedom is not the cause of a race or a sect, a party or a class—it is the cause of human kind, the very birthright of humanity.

Bullies are always cowards at heart and may be credited with a pretty safe instinct in scenting their prey.

Woman, Mother—your responsibility is one that might make angels tremble and fear to take hold!

Bill Cosby

Born 1937 ◆ comedian, writer, actor, and TV personality ◆ winner
of several Emmys and Grammys ◆ books include *Fatherhood* and
Love and Marriage

I don't know the key to success, but I know the key to failure is trying to please everybody.

A word to the wise ain't necessary—it's the stupid ones who need advice.

It isn't a matter of black is beautiful as much as it is white is not *all* that's beautiful.

I try to keep my humor away from the specific "black" and make it pertain to the general "human."

Always end the name of your child with a vowel, so that when you yell, the name will carry.

Human beings are the only creatures on earth that allow their children to come back home.

I recently turned fifty, which is young for a tree, midlife for an elephant, and ancient for a quarter-miler, whose son now says, "Dad, I just can't run the quarter with you anymore unless I bring something to read."

Let us now set forth one of the fundamental truths about marriage: the wife is in charge.

Women don't want to hear what you think. Women want to hear what they think—in a deeper voice.

The heart of marriage is memories; and if the two of you happen to have the same ones and can savor your reruns, then your marriage is a gift from the gods.

I am certainly not an authority on love because there are no authorities on love, just those who've had luck with it and those who haven't.

Sex education may be a good idea in the schools, but I don't believe the kids should be given homework.

Every closed eye is not sleeping, and every open eye is not seeing.

Gray hair is God's graffiti.

The past is a ghost, the future a dream, and all we ever *have* is now.

Alexander Crummell

1819–1898 ◆ minister, educator, lecturer, essayist, and scholar
◆ early advocate of black nationalism ◆ founder of the
American Negro Academy

We are Americans. We were born in no foreign clime. Here, where we behold the noble rivers and the rich fields, and the healthful skies that may be called America; here, amid the institutions that now surround us, we first beheld the light of the impartial sun.

Cheapness characterizes almost all the donations of the American people to the Negro . . . cheap wages and cheap food, cheap and rotten huts; cheap and dilapidated schools; cheap and stinted weeks of schooling; cheap meeting houses for worship; cheap and ignorant ministers; cheap theological training; and now, cheap learning, culture and civilization!

There is no repugnance to the Negro buffoon, and the Negro scullion; but so soon as the Negro stands forth as an intellectual being, this toad of American prejudice, as at the touch of Ithuriel's spear, starts up a devil!

It is a sad reflection . . . that a sense of responsibility which comes with power is the rarest of things.

Error moves with quick feet and truth must never be lagging behind.

Countee Cullen

1903–1946 ◆ poet, writer, playwright, translator, and educator
◆ Harlem Renaissance notable ◆ books include *Color* and
Copper Sun

If I am going to be a poet at all, I am going to be POET and not NEGRO POET.

My chief problem has been that of reconciling a Christian upbringing with a pagan inclination.

We must be one thing or the other, an asset or a liability, the sinew in your wing to help you soar, or the chain to bind you to earth.

My poetry, I should think, has become the way of my giving out what music is within me.

There is no secret to success except hard work and getting something indefinable which we called the "breaks." In order for a writer to succeed, I suggest three things—read and write—and wait.

Evelyn Cunningham

1916–2010 ✦ journalist, radio show host, community activist, administrator, and feminist ✦ reporter and editor for *The Pittsburgh Courier* best known for her fearless civil rights era reportage ✦ helped establish the National Coalition of 100 Black Women

Each one of my husbands tried to diminish my independence and my work. They all loved me most while I was cooking—and I am not a good cook.

My parents wanted so much more for my brother . . . and I. No way we were going to pick cotton. We moved to Harlem where African Americans were progressive.

Paris is beautiful in the spring, but so is Harlem. Harlem is my home, and I will never leave it.

I think we find happiness in retrospect. We don't recognize it at the moment.

Women are the only oppressed group in our society that lives in intimate association with their oppressors.

Angela Davis

Born 1944 ✦ political activist, writer, and educator ✦ as a victim of political oppression during the early 1970s, she made it onto the FBI's "Ten Most Wanted List" ✦ autobiography, *Angela Davis*

We, the black women of today, must accept the full weight of a legacy wrought in blood by our mothers in chains . . . as heirs to a tradition of supreme perseverance and heroic resistance.

We know that the road to freedom has always been stalked by death.

Progressive art can assist people to learn not only about the objective forces at work in the society in which they live, but also about the intensely social character of their interior lives. Ultimately, it can propel people toward social emancipation.

Jails and prisons are designed to break human beings, to convert the population into specimens in a zoo—obedient to our keepers, but dangerous to each other.

[on her fugitive experience] Thousands of my ancestors had waited, as I had done, for nightfall to cover their steps, had leaned on one true friend to help them, had felt, as I did, the very teeth of the dogs at their heels. It was simple. I had to be worthy of them.

When white people are indiscriminately viewed as the enemy, it is virtually impossible to develop a political solution.

"Justifiable Homicide"—these innocuously official words conjured up the untold numbers of unavenged murders of my people.

In the act of resistance the rudiments of freedom are already present.

It is both humiliating and humbling to discover that a single generation after the events that constructed me as a public personality, I am remembered as a hairdo.

Miles Davis

1926–1991 ◆ jazz trumpeter, composer, and recording artist
◆ modern jazz icon ◆ albums include *Birth of the Cool*,
Bitches Brew, and *Kind of Blue* ◆ autobiography, *Miles*

Bebop was about change, about evolution. It wasn't about standing still and becoming safe. If anybody wants to keep creating they have to be about change.

I've always told the musicians in my band to play what they *know* and then play *above that*. Because then anything can happen, and that's where great art and music happens.

I have always thought that narcotics should be legalized so that it wouldn't be that much of a street problem.

They ought to pick more fair-minded people to be police officers, because the job's too important to have any kind of racist white person walking around with a gun and a license to kill.

For me, music and life are all about style.

Ossie Davis

1917–2005 ♦ stage, screen, and TV actor, director, writer, and playwright ♦ films include *Cotton Comes to Harlem*, his directorial debut ♦ books include *Just Like Martin* and with his wife, Ruby Dee, *Life Lit by Some Large Vision: Selected Speeches and Writings*

I find in being black, a thing of beauty: a joy, a strength; a secret cup of gladness, a native land in neither time nor space, a native land in every Negro face! Be loyal to yourselves: your skin, your hair, your lips, your Southern speech, your laughing kindness, your Negro kingdoms, vast as any other.

Acting and preaching are essentially the same . . . The theater is a church and I consider myself as part of an institution that has an obligation to teach about Americanism, our culture and morals.

Any form of art is a form of power; it has impact, it can affect change—it can not only move us, it makes us move.

Mom and dad would tell . . . humorous tales of their own escapades. They took life and broke it up in little pieces and fed it to us like little birds. I think I always knew what I wanted to do. I went to school to learn to write.

Like exercise strengthens the body, struggle strengthens the character.

Material deprivation is horrible, but it does not compare to spiritual deprivation.

I can move between . . . different disciplines because I am essentially a storyteller, and the story I want to tell is about black people. Sometimes I sing the story, sometimes I dance it, sometimes I tell tales about it, but I always want to share my great satisfaction at being a black man at this time in history.

Sammy Davis, Jr.

1925–1990 ♦ singer, dancer, comedian, and actor with vaudeville roots ♦ winner of multiple Grammy and Emmy awards ♦ hit songs include "Mr. Bojangles," "I've Gotta Be Me," and "Candy Man" ♦ autobiography, *Yes, I Can!*

Talk about handicap—I'm a one-eyed Negro Jew.

Ten or fifteen years ago, you could tell the brothers from the cousins. Not anymore. Everybody [sounds] black—except John Denver.

Being a star made it possible for me to get insulted in places where the average Negro could never hope to go and get insulted.

Alcohol gives you infinite patience for stupidity.

All I really had was my talent. Without that I wouldn't be welcome at the White House.

Fame comes with its own standard. A guy who twitches his lips is just another guy with a lip twitch—unless he's Humphrey Bogart.

I have to be a star like another man has to breathe.

My manic pursuit of success cost me everything I could love: my wife, my three children, some friends I would have liked to grow old with.

If you want to be the best . . . you've got to work harder than anybody else.

The ultimate mystery is one's own self.

Ruby Dee

Born 1924 ◆ stage, screen, TV actress, and civil rights activist
◆ films include *The Jackie Robinson Story, A Raisin in the Sun*
and *Do the Right Thing* ◆ books include *My One Good Nerve*,
and *With Ossie and Ruby: In This Life Together* (co-authored with
her husband)

God, make me so uncomfortable that I will do the very thing I fear.

The greatest gift is not being afraid to question.

The kind of beauty I want most is the hard-to-get kind that comes from within—strength, courage, dignity.

Martin R. Delaney

1812–1885 ◆ abolitionist, lecturer, community leader, writer, and
newspaper editor ◆ an early advocate of black nationalism ◆ author
of one of the first African-American novels published in the U.S.—
Blake, or the Huts of Africa

A child born under oppression has all the elements of servility in its constitution.

A serpent is a serpent, and none the less a viper, because nestled in the bosom of an honest hearted man.

One thing is certain; our Elevation is the work of our own hands.

Every people should be the originators of their own designs, the projector of their own schemes, and creators of the events that lead to their destiny—the consummation of their desires.

One of our great temporal curses is our consummate poverty. We are the poorest people, as a class, in the world of civilized mankind—abjectly, miserably poor, no one scarcely being able to assist the other. To this, of course, there are noble exceptions; but that which is common to, and the very process by which white men exist, and succeed in life, is unknown to colored men in general.

We must MAKE an ISSUE, CREATE an EVENT, and ESTABLISH a NATIONAL POSITION for OURSELVES; and never may expect to be respected as men and women, until we have undertaken some fearless, bold, and adventurous deeds of daring—contending against every odds—regardless of every consequence.

Bessie (Annie Elizabeth) Delany

1891–1995 ◆ dentist, civil rights activist, and writer who lived to be 104 ◆ the second African-American female dentist licensed in New York State ◆ with her sister Sadie, she co-wrote *Having Our Say: The Delany Sisters' First 100 Years* (produced as a play) and *The Delany Sisters' Book of Everyday Wisdom*

I thought I could change the world. It took me a hundred years to figure out I *can't* change the world. I can only change Bessie. And honey, that ain't easy either.

I can't imagine having so little faith in the Lord, and so much faith in money, that you would end your life over a little thing like losing your fortune.

When people ask me how we've lived past 100, I say "Honey, we were never married. We never had husbands to worry us to death." . . . In those days, a man expected you to be in charge of a perfect household, to look after his every need. Honey, I wasn't interested.

When you get real old, honey, you realize there are certain things that just don't matter anymore. You lay it all on the table. There's a saying: Only little children and old folks tell the truth.

Money is at the root of every mess you can think of, including slavery.

Ain't nobody going to censor *me*, no, sir! I'm a 101 years old, and at my age, honey, I can say what I want!

Even with all my wrinkles! I am beautiful!

Sadie (Sarah Louise) Delany

1889–1999 ◆ educator, civil rights activist, and writer ◆ lived to be 109 ◆ memoir, *On My Own at 107: Reflections on Life Without Bessie*

Life is short, and it's up to you to make it sweet.

In our dreams, we are always young.

Samuel R. Delany

Born 1942 ◆ writer, educator, and literary critic ◆ best known for his award-winning science fiction works ◆ nephew of the Delany sisters ◆ books include *The Einstein Intersection, Dahlgren,* and *The Jewels of Aptor*

The only important elements in any society are the artistic and the criminal, because they alone, by questioning the society's values, can force it to change.

The General Public is a statistical fiction created by a few exceptional men to make the loneliness of being exceptional a little easier to bear.

The racial situation, permeable as it might sometimes seem (and it is, yes, highly permeable), is nevertheless your total surround.

The factors controlling a writer's popularity are as mysterious and ultimately as unknowable as the number of stars in the sky.

David Dinkins

Born 1927 ◆ politician, educator, and humanitarian ◆ Manhattan
borough president and first African-American mayor of
New York City

You can believe that almost any black who holds office or aspires to
office is obliged to have a view on controversial black figures. I'd like
to be asked about controversial white figures for a change.

Race relations can be an appropriate issue . . . but only if you want
to craft solutions, and not catalogue complaints.

I stand before you today as the elected leader of the greatest city of a
great nation, to which my ancestors were brought, chained and
whipped, in the hold of a slave ship. We have not finished the journey
toward liberty and justice, but surely we have come a long way.

You can be anything you want to be. You can be a street sweeper, if
you want. Just be the best blasted street sweeper you can be . . . And,
you *know* you can be mayor.

Little dreams stay home. Big dreams go to New York.

Frederick Douglass

1818–1895 ◆ writer, abolitionist, orator, and women's rights
advocate ◆ ex-slave who became a leader in the antislavery
movement of the 1800s, laying the foundation for the civil rights
era of the twentieth century ◆ autobiography, *Narrative of the Life
of Frederick Douglass, An American Slave*

You have seen how a man was made a slave; you shall see how a
slave was made a man.

It seems to me that the colored man has now almost as much need
of a faithful advocate as in the time of slavery. Though no longer
bought and sold in the market we are still a proscribed, oppressed
and maltreated race at nearly all points.

There is not a breeze that sweeps to us from the South, but comes
laden with the wail of our suffering people. . . . The American
people are once more being urged to do from necessity what they
should have done from a sense of right, and of sound statesmanship.
It is the same old posture of affairs, wherein our rulers do wrong
from choice and right from necessity.

This government will not have done its duty until a school-house is placed at every cross-road of the South and a bayonet between every ballot-box.

If there is no struggle, there is no progress. Those who profess to favor freedom and yet deprecate agitation, are men who want crops without plowing up the ground, they want rain without thunder and lightning. They want the ocean without the awful roar of its many waters.

The doctrine that submission to violence is the best cure for violence did not hold good as between slaves and overseers. He was whipped oftener who was whipped easiest.

We are free to say that in respect to political rights, we hold women to be justly entitled to all we claim for men.

The mean and cowardly assault [the Negro] because they know that his friends are few.

A man without force is without the essential dignity of humanity. Human nature is so constituted, that it cannot honor a helpless man, though it can pity him, and even this it cannot do long if signs of power do not arise.

Power concedes nothing without a demand. It never did and it never will. . . . The limits of tyrants are prescribed by the endurance of those whom they oppress.

Of my father I know nothing. Slavery had no recognition of fathers, as none of families.

To the lawyer, the preacher, the politician, and to the man of letters, there is no neutral ground. He that is not for us, is against us.

Slaves were expected to sing as well as to work. A silent slave was not liked, either by masters or overseers.

You degrade us and then ask why we are degraded—you shut our mouths, and then ask why we don't speak—you close your colleges and seminaries against us, and then ask why we don't know more.

What, to the American slave, is your Fourth of July? I answer: a day that reveals to him, more than all other days of the year, the gross injustice and cruelty to which he is the constant victim. To him your celebration is a sham . . . a thin veil to cover up crimes which would disgrace a nation of savages.

The songs of the slaves present the sorrows, rather than the joys, of his heart; and he is relieved by them, only as an aching heart is relieved by its tears. . . . Sorrow and desolation have their songs, as well as joy and peace. Slaves sing more to *make* themselves happy, than to express their happiness.

In coming to a fixed determination to run away, we did more than Patrick Henry when he resolved upon liberty or death. With us it was a doubtful liberty at most, and almost certain death if we failed. For my part, I should prefer death to hopeless bondage.

We want to live in the land of our birth, and to lay our bones by the side of our fathers'; and nothing short of an intense love of personal freedom keeps us from the South. For the sake of this, most of us would live on a crust of bread and a cup of water.

The Negro was not a coward at Bunker Hill; he was not a coward in Haiti; he was not a coward in the late war for the Union; he was not a coward at Harpers Ferry, with John Brown; and care should be taken against goading him to acts of desperation by continuing to punish him for heinous crimes of which he is not legally convicted.

The sin against the Negro is both sectional and national, and until the voice of the North shall be heard in emphatic condemnation and withering reproach against those continued ruthless mob-law murders, it will remain equally involved with the South in this common crime.

Weeds do not more naturally spring out of a manure pile than crime out of enforced destitution.

The very crimes of slavery become slavery's best defense. By making the enslaved a character fit only for slavery, they excuse themselves for refusing to make the slave a freeman.

A little learning, indeed, may be a dangerous thing, but the want of learning is a calamity to any people.

No man can put a chain about the ankle of his fellow man, without at least finding the other end of it about his own neck.

Rita Dove

Born 1952 ◆ poet, writer, and educator ◆ winner of the Pulitzer
Prize for Poetry ◆ first African-American poet laureate of the U.S.
◆ books include *Thomas and Beulah*, *The Yellow House on the
Corner*, and *Mother Love*

The mind does not take its complexion from the skin.

For many years, I thought a poem was a whisper overheard, not an
aria heard.

Under adversity, under oppression, the words begin to fail, the easy
words begin to fail. In order to convey things accurately, the human
being is forced to find the most precise words possible, which is a
precondition for literature.

I try to show what it is about language and music that enthralls,
because I think those are the two elements of poetry.

Poetry is language at its most distilled and most powerful.

There are ways to make of the moment a topiary so the pleasure's in
walking through.

Who discovered usefulness? Who forgot how to sing, simply?

My parents instilled in us the feeling that learning was the most
exciting thing that could happen to you, and it never ends.

W. E. B. Du Bois

1868–1963 ◆ writer, educator, social scientist, scholar, and
civil rights activist ◆ pioneer in the field of black studies ◆ Harlem
Renaissance notable ◆ director of publicity for the NAACP, and
founder and editor of its magazine, *The Crisis* ◆ best-known book,
The Souls of Black Folk

The problem of the Twentieth Century is the problem of the color
line.

No one but a Negro going into the South without previous experience of color caste can have any conception of its barbarism.

The cost of liberty is less than the price of repression.

Democracy is not a gift of power, but a reservoir of knowledge.

One ever feels his twoness—an American, a Negro; two souls, two thoughts, two unreconciled strivings; two warring ideals in one dark body, whose dogged strength alone keeps it from being torn asunder.

To the ordinary American or Englishman, the race question at bottom is simply a matter of ownership of women; white men want the right to use all women, colored and white, and they resent the intrusion of colored men in this domain.

The future woman must have a life work and economic independence. She must have the right of motherhood at her own discretion.

But what of black women? . . . I most sincerely doubt if any other race of women could have brought its fineness up through so devilish a fire.

Negro art is today plowing a difficult row. We want everything that is said about us to tell of the best and highest and noblest in us. We insist that our Art and Propaganda be one. We fear that evil in us will be called racial, while in others it is viewed as individual. We fear that our shortcomings are not merely human.

The South believed an educated Negro to be a dangerous Negro. And the South was not wholly wrong; for education among all kinds of men always has had, and always will have, an element of danger and revolution, of dissatisfaction and discontent.

There was scarcely a white man in the South who did not honestly regard Emancipation as a crime, and its practical nullification as a duty.

The greatest and most immediate danger of white culture is its fear of the truth, its childish belief in the efficacy of lies as a method of human uplift.

However laudable an ambition to rise may be, the first duty of an upper class is to serve the lower classes. The aristocracies of all peoples have been slow in learning this and perhaps the Negro is no slower than the rest, but his peculiar situation demands that in his case this lesson be learned sooner.

There is in this world no such force as the force of a man determined to rise. The human soul cannot be permanently chained.

All art is propaganda and ever must be, despite the wailing of the purists. I stand in utter shamelessness and say that whatever art I have for writing has been used always for propaganda for gaining the right of black folk to love and enjoy. I do not care a damn for any art that is not used for propaganda. But I do care when propaganda is confined to one side while the other is stripped and silent.

Until the art of the black folk compels recognition they will not be rated as human.

Sit no longer blind, Lord God, deaf to our prayer and dumb to our dumb suffering. Surely Thou too are not white, O Lord, a pale, bloodless, heartless thing?

Paul Laurence Dunbar

1872–1906 ◆ poet, writer, and lyricist ◆ first African-American poet to garner a national audience ◆ books include *Lyrics of Lowly Life* and *The Sport of the Gods* ◆ wrote the libretto and lyrics for the black musical *Clorindy; or, The Origin of the Cake Walk*, the first all-black show to play on Broadway

We wear the mask that grins and lies.

Whether the race be white or black, political virtue is always in a minority.

In politics we are all lambs and the wolves are only to be found in the other party.

Men talk of the Negro problem; there is no Negro problem. The problem is whether American people have loyalty enough, honor enough, patriotism enough, to live up to their own Constitution.

We Negroes love our country. We fought for it. We ask only that we be treated as well as those who fought against it.

People are taking it for granted that [the Negro] ought not to work with his head. And it is so easy for these people among whom we are living to believe this; it flatters and satisfies their self-complacency.

Money is a great dignifier.

I know why thc caged bird sings, ah me, when his wing is bruised and his bosom sore, when he beats his bars and he would be free; it is not a carol of joy or glee, but a prayer that he sends from his heart's deep core.

Alice Dunbar-Nelson

1875–1935 ◆ poet, writer, and educator ◆ books include
Violets and Other Tales and *The Goodness of Saint Roque and Other Stories*

I sit and sew—a useless task it sccms, my hands grown tired, my head weighed down with dreams.

It's punishment to be compelled to do what one doesn't wish.

In every race, in every nation, and in every clime in every period of history there is always an eager-eyed group of youthful patriots who seriously set themselves to right the wrongs done to their racc, or nation or sect, or sometimes to art or self-expression. No race or nation can advance without them.

Katherine Dunham

c. 1909–2006 ◆ dancer, choreographer, anthropologist, and social
activist ◆ major innovator in African-American modern dance, and
leader in the field of ethnochoreology (the study of folk dance) who
cicated the gcnre of Afro-Caribbean dance ◆ memoir,
A Touch of Innocence: Memoirs of Childhood

I used to want the words "She tried" on my tombstone. Now I want "She did it."

There is a purifying process in dancing.

We weren't pushing black is beautiful. We just showed it.

Start somcthing else [besides career] that makes use of your creative ability, because if you don't you will die inside as a person.

Go within every day and find the inner strength so that the world will not blow your candle out.

Michael Eric Dyson

Born 1958 ✦ writer, educator, minister, TV and radio
commentator, and scholar ✦ ex-gang member and "hip-hop
intellectual" ✦ books include *Between God and Gangsta Rap* and
Why I Love Black Women

[Rosa Parks] sat down with dignity so that all black people could
stand up with pride.

When we love black women, we love ourselves, and the God who
made us.

Black women have learned, more successfully than black men, to
absorb the pain of their predicament and to keep stepping.

Gangsta rap often reaches higher than its ugliest, lowest common
denominator . . . At its best, this music draws attention to complex
dimensions of ghetto life ignored by most Americans. . . . Indeed,
gangsta rap's in-your-face style may do more to force America to
confront crucial social problems than a million sermons or political
speeches.

Unfortunately, the prisons of our land often reproduce the pathology
that they seek to eliminate.

For black folk who have too often been dismissed, stigmatized, or
silenced without a hearing, we should be wary of repeating such
rituals of repression on our own kids.

Marian Wright Edelman

Born 1939 ✦ attorney, writer, and social activist ✦ headed NAACP
Legal Defense and Educational Fund and founded the
Children's Defense Fund ✦ recipient of an Albert Schweitzer
Humanitarian Award ✦ books include *The Measure of Our Success*
and *Lanterns: A Memoir of Mentors*

Somehow we are going to have to develop a concept of *enough* for
those at the top and at the bottom so that the necessities of the many
are not sacrificed for the luxury of the few.

Parents have become so convinced that educators know what is best
for children that they forget that they themselves are really the
experts.

If you are a parent, recognize that it is the most important calling and rewarding challenge you have. What you do every day, what you say and how you act, will do more to shape the future of America than any other factor.

God did not create two classes of children or human beings—only one.

White Anglo-Saxon males never have felt inferior as a result of their centuries of "affirmative action" and quotas . . . in jobs from which Jews, racial minorities, and women were excluded and too often still are.

People who don't vote have no line of credit with people who are elected and thus pose no threat to those who act against our interests.

Never work just for money or for power. They won't save your soul or help you sleep at night.

Service is the rent we pay for living. It is the very purpose of life and not something you do in your spare time.

First World privilege and Third World deprivation and rage are struggling to coexist not only in our nation's capital but all over an America that has the capacity but not the moral commitment and political will to protect all its young. . . . We need to stop punishing children because we don't like their parents.

It's a spiritually impoverished nation that permits infants and children to be the poorest Americans.

All of our Mercedes Benzes and Halston frocks will not hide our essential failure as a generation of black "haves" who did not protect the black future during our watch.

The question is not whether we can afford to invest in every child; it is whether we can afford not to.

What unites us is far greater than what divides us as families and friends and Americans and spiritual sojourners on this Earth.

Speak truth to power.

Joycelyn Elders

Born 1933 ◆ pediatrician and public health administrator ◆ first
African American to hold the office of surgeon general of the U.S.
◆ autobiography, *Joycelyn Elders, M.D.: From Sharecropper's
Daughter to Surgeon General*

[On sex education] We've tried ignorance for a thousand years. It's
time we try education.

We taught them what to do in the front seat of a car. Now it's time
to teach them what to do in the back seat.

As long as I was in Washington I never met anybody that I thought
was good enough, who knew enough, or who loved enough to make
sexual decisions for anybody else.

If you can't control your reproduction, you can't control your life.

Condoms will break, but I can assure you that vows of abstinence
will break more easily than condoms.

[Anti-abortionists] love little babies as long as they are in somebody
else's uterus.

We really need to get over this love affair with the fetus and start
worrying about children.

Once I had a professor say to me, "You know, you have as much
education as a lot of white people." I said, "Doctor, I have more
education than most white people."

You can't be what you don't see. I didn't think about being a doctor.
I didn't even think about being a clerk in a store, I'd never seen a
black clerk in a clothing store.

There's a great big difference between being concerned and being
committed. When you're concerned, it's negotiable. When I went
to Washington, I was committed. And what I was about was not
negotiable.

I came to Washington as prime steak, and after being there a little
while I feel like low-grade hamburger.

Duke Ellington

1899–1974 ◆ jazz pianist, composer, arranger, and bandleader
◆ compositions include "Mood Indigo," "In a Sentimental Mood,"
and "It Don't Mean a Thing (If It Ain't Got That Swing)"
◆ autobiography, *Music Is My Mistress*

By and large, jazz has always been like the kind of man you wouldn't want your daughter to associate with.

The common root [for jazz, blues, ragtime, swing, and bop], of course, comes out of Africa. That's the pulse. The African pulse.

Every intersection in the road of life is an opportunity to make a decision, and at some I had only to listen.

A man is a god in ruins.

Every man prays in his own language, and there is no language that God does not understand.

I merely took the energy it takes to pout and wrote some blues.

You've got to find some way of saying it without saying it.

Jazz is above all a total freedom to express oneself.

Critics have their purposes, and they're supposed to do what they do, but sometimes they get a little carried away with what they think someone should have done, rather than concerning themselves with what they did.

The ultimate in art is self-expression, not escape.

People making a living doing something they don't enjoy wouldn't even be happy with a one-day work week.

Life has two rules: Number 1, never quit! Number 2, always remember rule number 1.

Music is my mistress and she plays second fiddle to no one.

Ralph Ellison

1914–1994 ◆ writer, educator, scholar, and editor ◆ literary icon
◆ his first novel *Invisible Man* won the National Book Award ◆
other books include *Shadow and Act* and *Going to the Territory*

When I discover who I am, I'll be free.

I am not ashamed of my grandparents for having been slaves. I am only ashamed of myself for having at one time been ashamed.

There are few things in the world as dangerous as sleepwalkers.

I am an invisible man. . . . I am a man of substance, of flesh and bone, fiber and liquids—and I might even be said to possess a mind. I am invisible, understand, simply because people refuse to see me.

Life is to be lived, not controlled, and humanity is won by continuing to play in face of certain defeat.

If the word has the potency to revive and make us free, it has the power to blind, imprison, and destroy.

The understanding of art depends finally upon one's willingness to extend one's humanity and one's knowledge of human life.

[School] dropouts are living critics of their environment, of our society, and of our educational system.

Cultural pluralism: it's the air we breathe; it's the ground we stand on.

Harlem is a place where our folklore is preserved and transformed. It is the place where the body of our Negro myth and legend thrives. It is a place where our styles, musical styles, the many styles of Negro life, find continuity and metamorphosis.

There must be possible a fiction which, leaving sociology and case histories to the scientists, can arrive at the truth about the human condition, here and now, with all the bright magic of the fairy tale.

Medgar Evers

1925–1963 ◆ civil rights activist ◆ as the first Mississippi field
secretary for the NAACP, he worked tirelessly and courageously to
bring the murderers of Emmett Till to justice ◆ one of the first
martyrs of the civil rights movement (assassinated in 1963)
◆ he inspired a new motto for the movement:
"After Medgar, no more fear."

Our only hope is to control the vote.

I'm looking to be shot any time I step out of my car. . . . If I die, it
will be in a good cause. I've been fighting for America just as much
as the soldiers in Vietnam.

You shouldn't hate white people. You shouldn't hate anyone. That's
no way to live.

You can kill a man, but you can't kill an idea.

Myrlie Evers-Williams

Born 1933 ◆ civil rights activist ◆ first woman elected to chair the
NAACP ◆ first African-American woman to serve on the Los
Angeles Board of Public Works ◆ books include *The Autobiography
of Medgar Evers: A Hero's Life and Legacy Revealed Through His
Writings, Letters, and Speeches*

[The Till case] touched off the worldwide clamor and cast the glare
of a world spotlight on Mississippi's racism. . . . For it was the proof
that even youth was no defense against the ultimate terror, that
lynching was still the final means by which white supremacy would
be upheld, that whites could still murder Negroes with impunity, . . .
that no Negro's life was really safe.

We both knew he was going to die. Medgar didn't want to be
a martyr. But if he had to die to get us that far, he was willing to
do it.

Perhaps Medgar did more in death than in life. But he lives on.

Louis Farrakhan

Born 1933 ◆ minister, civil rights activist, and classical violinist
◆ National Representative of the Nation of Islam ◆ author of
A Torchlight for America

My ministry is not a ministry of hate. It is a ministry of love. We are teaching our people to love themselves. We're tired of laying at the feet of the white people begging them to do for us what we can do for ourselves.

You've got to get the mind cleared out before you put the truth in it.

I used to hate. But as I've matured in the word of God, I now see that hatred has no place here.

Never exalt people because they're in your family; never exalt people because they're your color; never exalt people because they're your kinfolk. Exalt them because they're worthy.

You must recognize that the way to get the good out of your brother and your sister is not to return evil for evil.

Black leadership has to recognize that principles more than speech, character more than a claim, is greater in advancing the cause of our liberation than what has transpired thus far.

Louis Farrakhan has become quite a controversial brother. . . . Once you speak against the popular version of the truth, then you must be willing to pay the price for so doing.

The problems we face as a nation are indeed, at the root, spiritual.

It is easy to do right out of fear, but it is better to do right because right is right.

Jessie Redmon Fauset

1882–1961 ◆ poet, writer, and editor ◆ Harlem Renaissance notable
◆ literary editor of *The Crisis* (journal of the NAACP)
◆ books include *There Is Confusion* and
Plum Bun; A Novel Without a Moral

It was a curious business, this color. It was the one god apparently to whom you could sacrifice everything.

All the possibilities of all black men are needed to weld together the black men of the world against the day when black and white meet to do battle. God grant that when that day comes we shall be so powerful that the enemy will say, "But behold! These men are our brothers."

New York, it appeared, had two visages. It could offer an aspect radiant with promise or a countenance lowering and forbidding. With its flattering possibilities it could elevate to the seventh heaven, or lower to the depths of hell with its crushing negations. And loneliness! Loneliness such as that offered by the great, noisy city could never be imagined.

The black man bringing gifts and particularly the gift of laughter . . . is easily the most anomalous, the most inscrutable figure of the century.

Men are always wanting women to give, but they don't want the women to want to give. They want to take—or at any rate compel the giving. . . . If we don't give enough we lose them. If we give too much we lose ourselves.

Ella Fitzgerald

1918–1996 ◆ "First Lady of Song" ◆ jazz and pop vocalist,
scat singer, song stylist, and bestselling recording artist ◆ her own
composition (with Al Feldman), "A-Tisket, A-Tasket," was her
first hit

The only thing better than singing is more singing.

I stole everything I ever heard, but mostly I stole from the horns.

Sometimes you can find you're way up on top and all by yourself. It can get pretty lonely up there, and you can miss all the licks.

Just don't give up trying to do what you really want to do. Where there is love and inspiration, I don't think you can go wrong.

It isn't where you come from; it's where you're going that counts.

George Foreman

Born 1949 ◆ boxer, preacher, and entrepreneur ◆ won an
Olympic gold medal and the world heavyweight crown
◆ autobiography, *By George*

We're all like blind men on a corner—we got to learn to trust people, or we'll never cross the street.

[on being a preacher] I don't even think about a retirement program because I'm working for the Lord, for the Almighty. And even though the Lord's pay isn't very high, his retirement program is, you might say, out of this world.

Everybody wants to be somebody. The thing you have to do is give them confidence they can. You have to give a kid a dream.

James Forten

1766–1842 ◆ abolitionist, inventor, businessman, and social activist ◆ worked as a powder boy during the Revolutionary War ◆ author of the pamphlet, A *Series of Letters by a Man of Colour*

Has the God who made the white man and the black left any record declaring us a different species? Are we not sustained by the same power, supported by the same food, hurt by the same wounds, wounded by the same wrongs, pleased with the same delights, and propagated by the same means? And should we not then enjoy the same liberty, and be protected by the same laws?

It seems almost incredible that the advocates of liberty should conceive of the idea of selling a fellow creature to slavery.

Many of our ancestors were brought here more than 100 years ago; many of our fathers, many of ourselves, have fought and bled for the independence of our country. Do not then expose us to sale. Let not the spirit of the father behold the son robbed of that liberty which he died to establish, but let the motto of our legislature be: "The law knows no distinction."

Timothy Thomas Fortune

1856–1928 ◆ poet, writer, orator, civil rights leader, and publisher ◆ helped organize the radical National Afro-American League ◆ books include *Black and White: Land, Labor, and Politics in the South*

The great newspapers, which should plead the cause of the oppressed and the downtrodden, which should be the palladiums of the people's rights, are all on the side of the oppressor or by silence preserve a dignified but ignominious neutrality. Day after day they weave a false picture of facts—facts which must measurably influence the future historian of the times in the composition of impartial history.

The real problem is not the Negro but the Nation.

The race cannot succeed, nor build strong citizens, until we have a race of women competent to do more than bear a brood of negative men.

We do not counsel violence, we counsel manly retaliation.

The sleepless agent of colonization . . . has penetrated the utmost bounds of the globe. It has wrenched from the weak their fertile valleys and luxuriant hillsides, and when they protested, when they resisted, it has enslaved them or cut their throats.

Mob law is the most forcible expression of an abnormal public opinion; it shows the society is rotten to the core.

When the Negro who steals from society what society steals from him under the specious cover of invidious law is hung upon the nearest oak tree, and the white villain who shoots a Negro without provocation is not so much as arrested—when society tolerates such an abnormal state of things, what will the harvest be?

It is bad enough to be denied equal political rights, but to be murdered by mobs—denied the protection of life and limb and property—the thing is not to be endured without protest, and if violence must be met with violence, let it be met.

As the agitation which culminated in the abolition of African slavery in this country covered a period of fifty years, so may we expect that before the rights conferred upon us by the war amendments are fully conceded, a full century will have passed away. . . . We have undertaken a serious work which will tax and exhaust the best intelligence and energy of the race for the next century.

The truth should be told, though it kill.

Redd Foxx

1922–1991 ◆ comedian, writer, film and TV actor ◆ best known as the star of *Sanford and Son* ◆ books include *The Redd Foxx Encyclopedia of Black Humor*

Beauty may be skin deep, but ugly goes clear to the bone.

When you see the handwriting on the wall, you're in the toilet.

Hey, leave the door open will ya? The flies haven't been out all day.

Health nuts are going to feel stupid someday, lying in hospitals dying of nothing.

There is no doubt that black street language has spilled over to every walk of life in our society today, thus making the American language that much more (if you'll pardon the expression) colorful.

Aretha Franklin

Born 1942 ◆ "Queen of Soul" ◆ award-winning singer-songwriter and pianist ◆ first woman inducted into the Rock and Roll Hall of Fame ◆ hits include "Respect," "(You Make Me Feel Like) A Natural Woman," and "Chain of Fools" ◆ autobiography, *Aretha: From These Roots*

I'm gonna make a gospel record and tell Jesus I cannot bear these burdens alone.

If a song's about something I've experienced or that could've happened to me, it's good. But if it's alien to me, I couldn't lend anything to it. Because that's what soul is all about.

I sing to people about what matters. I sing to the realists, people who accept it like it is. I express problems, there are tears when it's sad and smiles when it's happy. It seems simple to me, but to some, feelings take courage.

I believe that the black revolution certainly forced me and the majority of black people to begin taking a second look at themselves. It wasn't that we were all that ashamed of ourselves, we merely started appreciating our *natural* selves . . . falling in love with ourselves *just as we are.*

John Hope Franklin

1915–2009 ◆ writer and historian ◆ recipient of the Presidential Medal of Freedom ◆ books include the classic work, *From Slavery to Freedom*, and his autobiography, *Mirror to America*

It was necessary, as a black historian, to have a personal agenda.

If the house is to be set in order, one cannot begin with the present; he must begin with the past.

The white side has been in control of virtually everything, so they're the ones who need educating on what justice and equality mean.

The South's historians served the cause of Southern nationalism with more lasting effect than did its armies . . . Southerners must win with the pen what they had failed to win with the sword.

My challenge was to weave into the fabric of American history enough of the presence of blacks so that the story of the United States could be told adequately and fairly.

Racial segregation, discrimination, and degradation are no unanticipated accidents in this nation's history. They stem logically and directly from the legacy that the founding fathers bestowed upon contemporary America. . . . [W]hen the colonists emerged victorious from their war with England, they had both their independence and their slaves.

E. Franklin Frazier

1894–1962 ◆ sociologist, writer, and educator ◆ author of
The Negro Family in the United States, a groundbreaking work in
the field of sociology ◆ Harlem Renaissance notable ◆ other books
include *Black Bourgeoisie: The Rise of a New Middle Class in the
United States*

The Negro does not want love. He wants justice. . . . I believe it would be better for the Negro's soul to be seared with hate than dwarfed by self-abasement.

I am primarily interested in the Negro's self-respect. If the masses of Negroes can save their self-respect and remain free from hate, so much the better for their moral development.

The killing of a white man is always the signal for a kind of criminal justice resembling primitive tribal revenge.

The closer a Negro got to the ballot box, the more he looked like a rapist.

Education in the past has been too much inspiration and too little information.

Joe Frazier

Born 1944 ◆ "Smokin' Joe" ◆ boxer, singer, entrepreneur, and
fundraiser ◆ winner of an Olympic gold medal and the world
heavyweight title ◆ Boxing Hall of Fame ◆ autobiography, *Smokin'
Joe: The Autobiography of a Heavyweight Champion of the World*

Boxing is the only sport you can get your brain shook, your money
took and your name in the undertaker book.

You can map out a fight plan or a life plan, but when the action
starts it may not go the way you planned, and you're down to your
reflexes—which means your training. That's where your roadwork
shows. If you cheated on that in the dark of the mornin', well, you're
gettin' found out now under the bright lights.

Life doesn't run away from nobody. Life runs at people.

I don't want to knock my opponents out, I want to hit him, step
away, and watch him hurt. I want his heart.

*[comment made to Ali, his opponent, after their "Thriller in Manila"
bout]* You one bad nigger. We both bad niggers. We don't do no
crawlin'.

All I had to build my dream on was that homemade heavy bag.

Ernest J. Gaines

Born 1933 ◆ writer and educator ◆ books include his best-known
novel, *The Autobiography of Miss Jane Pittman*, *A Gathering of
Old Men*, and *A Lesson Before Dying*, which won a National Book
Critics Circle Award for fiction

I came from a place where people sat around and chewed sugarcane
and roasted sweet potatoes in the ashes and sat on ditch banks and
told tales and sat on porches and went into the swamps and went
into the fields—that's where I came from.

I have learned as much about writing about my people by listening
to blues and jazz and spirituals as I have by reading novels. The
understatements in the tenor saxophone of Lester Young, the crying,
haunting, forever searching sounds of John Coltrane, and the
softness and violence of Count Basie's big band—all have fired my
imagination as much as anything in literature.

Sometimes you got to hurt something to help something. Sometimes you have to plow under one thing in order for something else to grow.

There will always be men struggling to change, and there will always be those who are controlled by the past.

Henry Highland Garnet

1815–1882 ◆ writer, abolitionist, orator, educator, minister, and missionary ◆ one of the founders of the American and Foreign Antislavery Society ◆ advocate for colonization

You had better all die—die immediately, than live slaves, and entail your wretchedness upon your posterity.

Slavery had stretched its dark wings of death over the land, the Church stood silently by—the priests prophesied falsely, and the people loved to have it so. Its throne is established, and now it reins triumphant.

Millions have come from eternity into time, and have returned again to the world of spirits, cursed and ruined by American slavery.

Your dead fathers speak to you from their graves. Heaven, as with a voice of thunder, calls on you to arise from the dust. Let your motto be resistance! *Resistance!* RESISTANCE! No oppressed people have ever secured their liberty without resistance.

Liberty is a spirit sent from God and like its great Author is no respecter of persons.

Marcus Garvey

1887–1940 ◆ social activist, writer, and orator ◆ founder of the "Back to Africa" movement ◆ established a newspaper, *The Negro World* ◆ founder of the international Universal Negro Improvement Association ◆ co-founder of the African Orthodox Church

Africa for the Africans, at home and abroad.

A people without the knowledge of their past history, origin and culture is like a tree without roots.

I know of no national boundary where the Negro is concerned. The whole world is my province until Africa is free.

We should say to the millions who are in Africa to hold the fort, for we are coming 400 million strong.

Africa has been sleeping for centuries—not dead, only sleeping.

Our leader will not be a white man with a black heart, nor a black man with a white heart, but a black man with a black heart.

If you have no confidence in self, you are twice defeated in the race of life. With confidence, you have won even before you have started.

There is no force like success, and that is why the individual makes all effort to surround himself throughout life with the evidence of it; as of the individual, so should it be of the nation.

There is no sense in hate: it comes back to you; therefore make your history so laudable, magnificent, and untarnished that another generation will not seek to repay your seeds for the sins inflicted upon their fathers.

The only protection against injustice in man is power—physical, financial, and scientific.

Radicalism is a label that is always applied to the people who are endeavoring to get freedom.

Teach your children they are direct descendants of the greatest and proudest race who ever peopled the earth.

Take advantage of every opportunity; where there is none, make it for yourself.

A man's bread and butter is only insured when he works for it.

Black men are not going to cringe before anyone but God.

Let us not try to be the best or worst of others, but let us make the effort to be the best of ourselves.

The thing to do is to get organized; keep separated and you will be exploited, you will be robbed, you will be killed. Get organized and you will compel the world to respect you.

We must canonize our own saints, create our own martyrs, and elevate to positions of fame and honor black men and women who have made their distinct contributions to our racial history.

If others laugh at you, return the laughter to them; if they mimic you, return the compliment with equal force. . . . Honor them when they honor you, disrespect and disregard them when they vilely treat you. Their arrogance is but skin deep and an assumption that has no foundation in morals or in law.

We have outgrown slavery, but our minds are still enslaved to the thinking of the master race. Now take the kinks out of your mind, instead of out of your hair.

Henry Louis Gates, Jr.

Born 1950 ◆ writer, educator, scholar, literary critic, and editor ◆ the first African American to receive an Andrew W. Mellon Foundation Fellowship ◆ director of Harvard University's W. E. B. Du Bois Institute for African and African American Research ◆ books include *The Signifying Monkey, Loose Canons: Notes on the Culture Wars*, and his memoir, *Colored People*

My grandfather was colored, my father is Negro, and I am black.

The sad truth is that without complex business partnerships between African elites and European traders and commercial agents, the slave trade to the New World would have been impossible, at least on the scale it occurred.

Picasso's "Les Demoiselles d'Avignon"—the signature painting in the creation of Cubism—stands as a testament to the shaping influence of African sculpture and to the central role that African art played in the creation of modernism.

The African slave who sailed to the New World did not sail alone. People brought their culture, no matter how adverse the circumstances. And therefore part of America is African.

The creation of formal literature could be no mean matter in the life of the slave, since the sheer literacy of writing was the very commodity that separated animal from human being, slave from citizen, object from subject.

[Frederick] Douglass is our clearest example of the will to power as the will to write. The act of writing for the slave constituted the act of creating a public, historical self, not only the self of the individual author, but also the self, as it were, of the race.

In literacy lay freedom for the black slave. . . . No group of slaves anywhere, at any other period in history, has left such a large repository of testimony about the horror of becoming the legal property of another human being.

Classism and racism have been compounded together in a crucible so it's hard to know where one starts and where one stops.

Humanism starts not with identity but with the ability to identify with others. It asks what we have in common with others while acknowledging the internal diversity among ourselves. It is about the priority of a shared humanity.

What hurt me most about the glorious black awakening of the late and early seventies is that we lost our sense of humor. Many of us thought that enlightened politics excluded it.

That separateness led to inequality was the great theme of the civil rights era. That inequality leads to separateness is the unavoidable conclusion of its aftermath.

[rap lyrics on trial—obscenity or art?] The very large questions of obscenity and the First Amendment cannot even be addressed until those who would answer them become literate in the vernacular traditions of African Americans.

Mama and I would go to a funeral and she'd stand up to read the dead person's eulogy. She made the ignorant and ugly sound like scholars and movie stars, turned the mean and evil into saints and angels. She knew what people had meant to be in their hearts, not what the world had forced them to become. She knew the ways in which working too hard for paltry wages could turn you mean and cold, could kill the thing that had made you laugh.

Insofar as we, critics of the black tradition, master our craft, we serve both to preserve our own traditions and to shape their direction. All great writers demand great critics.

The last vestige of racism in the West will be intellectual racism.

Marvin Gaye

1939–1984 ◆ "Prince of Motown" ◆ singer-songwriter and drummer ◆ started with The Moonglows, a doo-wop group, and later became a solo recording artist for Motown ◆ hits include "How Sweet It Is (to Be Loved by You)," "What's Going On," and "Sexual Healing"

Music is one of the closest link-ups with God that we can probably experience. I think it's a common vibrating tone of the musical notes that holds all life together.

Most fear stems from sin; to limit one's sins, one must assuredly limit one's fear, thereby bringing more peace to one's spirit.

If you cannot find peace within yourself, you will never find it anywhere else.

[on Motown's 25th anniversary] Maybe today is the result of yesterday spent in wooden churches, singing the praises of our Maker in joyous harmony and love. Part of it has to be the songs we sang, working under the blazing sun, to help pass the hard times. Yesterday was also Bessie Smith, New Orleans, and gospel choirs, folk songs, Bojangles. Yesterday was the birthplace of today . . . songs of protest and anger, songs of gentleness and songs of wounds left unattended for far too long, songs to march to, to fly to, to make love to. It's music pure and simple and soulful.

Art is a way of possessing destiny.

I would like to be remembered as one of the twelve music disciples, and as a man who was aware and conscious of his environment, and as a person who was full of sensibility, erotic, profound.

Althea Gibson

1927–2003 ◆ "Jackie Robinson of Tennis" ◆ first African-American woman to be a competitor on the world tennis tour and the first to win a Grand Slam title ◆ autobiography, *I Always Wanted to Be Somebody*

I'm not a Negro tennis player. I'm a tennis player.

I always wanted to be somebody. If I made it, it's half because I was game enough to take a lot of punishment along the way, and half because there were a lot of people who cared enough to help me.

I knew that I was an unusual, talented girl through the grace of God. I didn't need to prove that to myself. I only wanted to prove it to my opponents.

In sports, you simply aren't considered a real champion until you have defended your title successfully. Winning it once can be a fluke; winning it twice proves you are the best.

People thought I was ruthless, which I was. I didn't give a darn who was on the other side of the net. I'd knock you down if you got in my way.

In the field of sports you are more or less accepted for what you do rather than what you are.

Bob Gibson

Born 1935 ◆ major league baseball player, coach, and TV
sportscaster ◆ Cy Young award-winner ◆ Baseball Hall of Fame
◆ autobiography, *From Ghetto to Glory*

A great catch is like watching girls go by—the last one you see is always the prettiest.

Why do I have to be an example for your kid? *You* be an example for your own kid.

I owe the public just one thing—a good performance.

I always got by on my ability. I never learned the politics of the game. I found out that honesty just pisses people off.

Have you ever thrown a ball 100 miles an hour? Everything hurts. Even your ass hurts.

The two most important things in life: good friends and a strong bullpen.

I wasn't throwing at them and they didn't know it, because they expected me to throw at somebody. So I never apologized. That's the worst thing in the world to do. You just stand out there like you did it on purpose.

When I was playing I never wished I was doing anything else. I think being a professional athlete is the finest thing a man can do.

[on his athletic prowess] It is not something I earned or acquired or bought. It is a gift. It is something that was given to me—just like the color of my skin.

Paula Giddings

Born 1947 ◆ writer, educator, feminist, and social historian
◆ books include *When and Where I Enter: The Impact of Black Women on Race and Sex in America* and *In Search of Sisterhood: Delta Sigma Theta and the Challenge of the Black Sorority Movement*

It was my mother who gave me my voice. She did this, I know now, by clearing a space where my words could fall, grow, then find their way to others.

What is at the summit of courage, I think, is freedom. The freedom that comes with the knowledge that no earthly thing can break you.

Throughout the social history of black women, children are more important than marriage in determining the woman's domestic role.

[The] fate of all blacks is inseparable by class. . . . The black middle class will remain fragile as long as there's a large and growing underclass.

[Black women] have been perceived as token women in black texts and token blacks in feminist ones.

I will write till I say goodbye to this world.

Dizzy Gillespie

1917–1993 ◆ jazz trumpeter and composer ◆ his career began with the Cab Calloway Orchestra ◆ during the 1940s he helped introduce the progressive jazz form known as bebop with saxophonist Charlie Parker ◆ pioneer in Afro-Cuban jazz

Be as you are and hope that it's right.

Freedom without organization is chaos. I want to put freedom into music the way I conceive it. It is free, but it's organized freedom.

Jazz was invented for people to dance to, we can't get away from that. My music calls more for listening, but it'll still make you shake your head and pat your feet. If I don't see anybody doing that in the audience, we ain't getting to them, and we're playing mostly for spirit, not for intellect.

Song and dance is a part of me. In high school I used to sing a song called "Goin' to Heaven on a Mule." I can't remember the song . . . but I used the philosophy behind it to build my act. The "mule" is my background in black folk culture and "heaven" is where I'm at.

Charlie Parker I hired, because he was undeniably a genius, musically, the other side of my heartbeat.

Fats Waller influenced me not only through his music, but his whole personality, because he was funny, and then you could sit him down at the piano and close his mouth and he'd play. This niggah could eat up a piano. Everybody respected him.

Comedy is important. As a performer, when you're trying to establish audience control, the best thing is to make them laugh if you can. That relaxes you more than anything.

I don't care too much about music. What I like is sounds.

Nikki Giovanni

Born 1943 ◆ poet, writer, social activist, lecturer, educator, and recording artist ◆ a major force in contemporary African-American poetry ◆ books include *Sacred Cows . . . and Other Edibles*, *Racism 101*, *Vacation Time: Poems for Children*, and *Cotton Candy on a Rainy Day*

Black love is black wealth.

If they kill me it won't stop the revolution.

It's not a ladder we're climbing, it's a literature we're producing. . . . We cannot possibly leave it to history as a discipline nor to sociology nor science nor economics to tell the story of our people.

The human spirit cannot be tamed and should not be trained.

Rappers are saying look at my life, look at what it's become. Kids have something to say and we should listen.

Deal with yourself as an individual worthy of respect and make everyone else deal with you the same way.

If you don't understand yourself you don't understand other people

Art is not for the cultivated taste. It is to cultivate taste.

Everything will change. The only question is growing up or decaying.

Mistakes are a fact of life. It's the response to the error that counts.

If you're a poet you are trying to teach. I think being in a classroom keeps you up to date. I think you'd miss a lot if all you did was meet other writers; if you never saw another generation.

Most of us love from our need to love, not because we find someone deserving.

Danny Glover

Born 1946 ◆ film, stage and TV actor, director, and political activist ◆ plays include *Master Harold . . . and the Boys* ◆ TV roles include *Mandela* ◆ films include *Places in the Heart, The Color Purple*, and *To Sleep with Anger*

Freedom Summer, the massive voter education project in Mississippi, was 1964. I graduated from high school in 1965. So becoming active was almost a rite of passage.

I have to be careful about the parts I take. Given how this industry has dealt with people like me, the parts I take have to be political choices.

If we talk about literacy, we have to talk about how to enhance our children's mastery over the tools needed to live intelligent, creative, and involved lives.

One of the main purveyors of violence in this world has been this country.

Every day of my life I walk with the idea I am black, no matter how successful I am.

Whoopi Goldberg

Born 1955 ◆ comedienne, writer, actor, TV personality, fundraiser,
and social activist ◆ films include *The Color Purple, Ghost* (for
which she won an Academy Award), and *Sister Act* ◆ books include
*Can I Be Honest with You?: A Practical Guide to Saying What You
Are Really Thinking* and her memoir, *Book*

I didn't dream about fame. I dreamed about getting my kid more
than one pair of shoes, or how to make $165 worth of groceries last
all month.

I took drugs because they were available to everyone in those times.
As everyone evolved into LSD, so did I. It was the time of Woodstock,
of be-ins and love-ins.

Junkies never know they have to stop and I don't know now how I
did. I'm the living legacy of this group of talented, wonderful dope
fiends who cleaned me up and made a lasting impression.

If every American donated five hours a week, it would equal the
labor of twenty million full-time volunteers.

I don't look like Halle Berry. But chances are, she's going to end up
looking like me.

I don't have pet peeves, I have whole kennels of irritation.

An actress can only play a woman. I'm an actor, I can play anything.

Work doesn't come to me; I go out and look for it.

Normal is in the eye of the beholder.

I am a humanist before anything—before I'm a Jew, before I'm
black, before I'm a woman. And my beliefs are for the human
race—they don't exclude anyone.

I've learned to take me for myself and to treat myself with a great
deal of love and a great deal of respect 'cause I like me. . . . I think
I'm kind of cool.

I grew up in a time when it would never have occurred to anyone to
tell me there was anything I couldn't do.

I am the American Dream. I am the epitome of what the American
Dream basically said. It said, you could come from anywhere and be
anything you want in this country. That's exactly what I've done.

Al Green

Born 1946 ◆ gospel and soul singer-songwriter, pastor, and humanitarian ◆ Songwriters Hall of Fame and the Gospel Hall of Fame ◆ hits include "Let's Stay Together," "Lean on Me," and "Tired of Being Alone" ◆ autobiography, *Take Me to the River*

I learned more stuff in church than I did in the world.

[on his earlier secular material] I know why I wrote those songs. I was a fornicator, an adulterer. The celestial will not mix with the terrestrial.

If I could live my life all over I'd do everything the same; the film in my camera would remain the same.

[on teaching children] Teach success before teaching responsibility. Teach them to believe in themselves. Teach them to think, "I'm not stupid." No child wants to fail. Everyone wants to succeed.

The music is the message, the message is the music. So that's my life ministry that the Big Man upstairs gave to me—a little ministry called love and happiness.

Dick Gregory

Born 1932 ◆ comedian, writer, social and anti-war activist, recording artist (comedy albums), and entrepreneur ◆ his social activism has focused on issues of world health and hunger ◆ books include his memoir, *Callus on My Soul,* and his autobiography, *Nigger*

[on breaking the color barrier in his early days as a comedian] I've got to go up there as an individual first, a Negro second. I've got to be a colored funny man, not a funny colored man.

The free man is the man with no fears.

Love is man's natural endowment, but he doesn't know how to use it. He refuses to recognize the power of love because of his love of power.

You know why Madison Avenue advertising has never done well in Harlem? We're the only ones who know what it means to be brand X.

We used to root for the Indians against the cavalry, because we didn't think it was fair in the history books that when the cavalry won it was a great victory, and when the Indians won it was a massacre.

I never believed in Santa Claus because I knew no white dude would come into my neighborhood after dark.

I never learned hate at home, or shame. I had to go to school for that.

If it wasn't for Abe Lincoln, I'd still be on the open market.

Riches do not delight us so much with their possession, as torment us with their loss.

When I lost my rifle, the Army charged me eighty-five dollars. That is why in the Navy the Captain goes down with the ship.

Just being a Negro doesn't qualify you to understand the race situation any more than being sick makes you an expert on medicine.

A real slave needs no chains.

How can I get justice from a judge who honestly does not know that he is prejudiced?

You gotta say this for whites, their self-confidence knows no bounds. Who else could go to a small island in the South Pacific, where there's no crime, poverty, unemployment, war or worry—and call it a primitive society.

Civil Rights: What black folks are given in the U.S. on the installment plan, as in civil rights bills. Not to be confused with human rights, which are dignity, stature, humanity, respect, and freedom belonging to all people by right of their birth.

It is dangerous for white America to insist that basic American documents be read by the black, poor, and oppressed, because such people are just naïve enough to go out and do what the founding fathers said oppressed people should do.

When you have a good mother and no father, God kind of sits in. It's not enough, but it helps.

Charlotte Forten Grimké

1837–1914 ◆ poet, writer, educator, missionary, and abolitionist ◆ her work was published in such periodicals as *The Liberator*, the *Anglo African magazine*, and the *Atlantic Monthly* ◆ best known for her *Bequest to Humanity*, a diary of her times

I wonder that every colored person is not a misanthrope. Surely we have everything to make us hate mankind.

Oh! It is hard to go through life meeting contempt with contempt, hatred with hatred, fearing, with too good reason, to love and trust hardly any one whose skin is white—however lovable, attractive, and congenial in seeming.

May those whose holy task it is, to guide impulsive youth, fail not to cherish in their souls a reverence for truth; for teachings which the lips impart must have their source within the heart.

[on the Emancipation Proclamation, January 1, 1863] Ah, what a grand, glorious day this has been. The dawn of freedom which it heralds may not break upon us at once; but it will surely come, and sooner, I believe, than we have ever dared hope before.

Francis J. Grimké

1850–1937 ◆ writer, minister, and civil rights activist ◆ helped
found the NAACP ◆ author of *The Negro: His Rights and Wrongs,
the Forces for Him and against Him*

The white people in this country seem to be greatly concerned as to whether humanity or the savage is to rule in other lands but utterly indifferent as to which rules in this.

[in 1918] The Negro soldier might just as well lay down his life here in defense of the principles of democracy as to go abroad to do so. . . . The greatest enemies to true democracy are not in Germany or Austria, but here in these United States of America.

The awful things that are going on in this nation—the wanton disregard of law, the exhibitions of brutality, of savagery—show, and show with a clearness which none can fail to see, that unless there comes to the Nation a greater emancipation than Lincoln's Proclamation effected, it is doomed, it is bound to go down.

Slavery is gone, but the spirit of it still remains.

It is only what is written upon the soul of man that will survive the wreck of time.

Lani Guinier

Born 1950 ◆ lawyer, educator, scholar, writer, and political activist
◆ the first African-American woman to achieve a tenured
professorship at Harvard Law School ◆ books include
*Lift Every Voice: Turning a Civil Rights Setback into
a New Vision of Social Justice* and *The Tyranny of the Majority*

In a racially divided society, majority rule may become majority tyranny.

I endured the personal humiliation of being vilified as the "madwoman" with the strange name, strange hair—you know what that means—and with the strange ideas. Those ideas being that all people deserve equal representation.

As soon as I started on voting rights, I knew that's what I wanted. It's not that I think I'm going to change the world, but I can do lawyer's work and the work of a sociologist. When you do voting rights . . . you know the community and you become kind of an organizer.

Democracy takes place when the silenced find a voice and when we begin to listen to what they have to say.

Alex Haley

1921–1992 ◆ writer and journalist ◆ best known for *Roots:
The Saga of an American Family*, his bestselling book about his
ten-year-long quest to learn his family's history, which became a TV
miniseries ◆ the book also won him the Pulitzer Prize and the
National Book Award ◆ collaborated with Malcolm X on the
Autobiography of Malcolm X

When you clench your fist, no one can put anything in your hand.

Here now in our swiftly paced technological era, it seems to me that not only younger black people, but we older ones as well, need urgently to show our living grandparents' generation that we do realize and respect and honor how much we have inherited and benefited because of the experiences which they have survived.

[on Malcolm X] I tried to be a dispassionate chronicler. But he was the most electric personality I have ever met, and I still can't quite conceive him dead. It still feels to me as if he has just gone into some next chapter, to be written by historians.

[*about* Roots] I acknowledge an immense debt to the griots* of Africa—where today it is rightly said that when a griot dies, it is as if a library has burned to the ground.

Arsenio Hall

Born 1955 ◆ actor, comedian, and TV personality ◆ films include
Coming to America and *Harlem Nights*

White America has always let us entertain them, but we've never had any real control, any real power. . . . It's a new day you know, and it's time for us to stop shooting the ball and start owning the court.

To be successful as a black man in this country, you have to be bicultural. White people can function in a white world and only concern themselves with white things. But a black man has to know it all.

Fannie Lou Hamer

1917–1977 ◆ civil rights and voting rights activist ◆ field secretary
for SNCC ◆ autobiography, *To Praise Our Bridges*

Whether you have a Ph.D., or a D.D. or no D., we're in this together. Whether you're from Morehouse or No house, we're in this bag together.

I'm sick and tired of being sick and tired.

White Americans today don't know what in the world to do because when they put us behind them, that's where they made their mistake. If they had put us in front, they wouldn't have let us look back. But they put us behind them, and we watched every move they made.

Only God has kept the Negro sane.

Nobody's free until everybody's free.

---

*[GRIOTS are storytellers of West Africa who preserve the oral histories of their people.]

I'd tell the white powers that I ain't trying to take nothing from them. I'm trying to make Mississippi a better place for all of us. And I'd say, "What you don't understand is that as long as you stand with your feet on my neck, you got to stand in a ditch, too. But if you move, I'm coming out. I want to get us both out of the ditch."

Black people know what white people mean when they say law and order.

What was the point of being scared? The only thing they could do to me was kill me and it seemed like they'd been trying to do that a little bit at a time ever since I could remember.

[on the treatment of activists] Is this America? The land of the free and the home of the brave? Where we have to sleep with our telephones off the hook, because our lives are threatened daily.

With the people, for the people, by the people. I crack up when I hear it; I say, with the handful, for the handful, by the handful, 'cause that's what really happens.

I used to think that if I could go North and tell people about the plight of black folk in the state of Mississippi everything would be all right. But traveling around I found one thing for sure: it's up-South and down-South, and it's no different.

If this is a great society, I'd hate to see a bad one.

Jupiter Hammon

1711–c. 1805 ♦ poet and writer ♦ the publication of his broadside
"An Evening Thought," a poem, made him the first African-
American writer to be published in America ♦ in 1786,
he delivered a speech containing his views on slavery before
the Africa Society in New York State

If we should ever get to Heaven, we shall find nobody to reproach us for being black, or for being slaves.

The Bible is a revelation of the mind and will of God to men. Therein we may learn what God is.

That liberty is a great thing we may know from our own feelings, and we may likewise judge so from the conduct of the white people, in the late [Revolutionary] war.

Fred Hampton

1948–1969 ◆ radical social activist ◆ a leader of the Black Panther
Party who was allegedly murdered by the FBI and the
Chicago Police

We understand that politics is nothing but war without bloodshed;
and war is nothing but politics with bloodshed.

What this country has done to nonviolent leaders like Martin Luther
King—I think that objectively says there's going to have to be an
armed struggle.

You can kill a revolutionary, but you cannot kill a revolution. You
can jail a liberation fighter, but you cannot jail liberation.

Lionel Hampton

1908–2002 ◆ "King of the Vibes" ◆ jazz vibraphonist, drummer,
piano, composer, and orchestra leader during the Big Band Era
◆ accolades include the Kennedy Center Lifetime Achievement
Award ◆ autobiography, *Hamp*

In those same towns where we couldn't get a hotel room or a meal
in a decent restaurant—even if we could pay for it—the people
treated us like kings once we got up on the stage.

With Benny [Goodman], touring with two black musicians was a
pioneering effort. Nobody had ever traveled with an integrated band
before, and even though Teddy Wilson and I were only part of the
Benny Goodman Quartet, that was still too much for some white
folks.

If you were a black entertainer of any kind—musician, singer,
comedian—being a headliner at the Apollo was your proudest
achievement.

It went from the classics to ragtime to Dixieland to swing to bebop
to cool jazz. . . . But it's always jazz. You can put a new dress on her,
a new hat on her, but no matter what kind of clothes you put on her,
she's the same old broad.

Music was our wife, and we loved her. And we stayed with her, and
we clothed her, and we put diamond rings on her hands.

W. C. Handy

1873–1958 ◆ "Father of the Blues" ◆ composer, musician, and
bandleader ◆ songs include "Memphis Blues" and "St. Louis Blues"
◆ co-owner of a music publishing company

Life is something like a trumpet. If you don't put anything in, you
won't get anything out.

The blues is where we came from and what we experience. The
blues came from nothingness, from want, from desire.

Sometimes I feel like nothin', somethin' throwed away, somethin'
throwed away. And then I get my guitar, play the blues all day.

Hard times that's all we hear 'round this way. Odd dimes they're
growing thinner each day. Good times, "just 'round the corner," so
they say.

In the South of long ago, whenever a new man appeared for work in
any of the laborers' gangs, he would be asked if he could sing. If he
could he got the job. The singing of these working men set the
rhythm for the work.

Modern blues is the expression of the emotional life of the race.

Lorraine Hansberry

1930–1965 ◆ playwright, poet, writer, public speaker, and civil
rights activist ◆ her best-known work, *A Raisin in the Sun*, was the
first play by an African-American woman produced on Broadway
◆ *To Be Young, Gifted and Black: Lorraine Hansberry
in Her Own Words*, was both a play and a book

Seems like God don't see fit to give the black man nothing but
dreams—but He did give us children to make them dreams seem
worthwhile.

The thing that makes you exceptional, if you are at all, is inevitably
that which must also make you lonely.

The foremost enemy of the Negro intelligentsia has been isolation.

The grim possibility is that she who "hides her brains" will, more
than likely, end up with a mate who is only equal to a woman with
"hidden brains" or none at all.

Obviously, the most oppressed of any oppressed group, will be its women.

[My grandmother] was born in slavery and had memories of it and they didn't sound anything like *Gone with the Wind*.

Perhaps we shall be the teachers when it is done. Out of the depths of pain we have thought to be our sole heritage in this world—O, we know about love! And that is why I say to you that, though it be a thrilling and marvelous thing to be merely young and gifted in such times, it is doubly so, doubly dynamic—to be young, gifted *and* black.

This is one of the glories of man, the inventiveness of the human mind and the human spirit: whenever life doesn't seem to give an answer, we create one.

I think that the human race does command its own destiny and that that destiny can eventually embrace the stars. If man is as small and ugly and grotesque as his most inhuman act, he is also as large as his most heroic gesture, and he is therefore a hero manyfold.

Never be afraid to a sit awhile and think.

Frances Ellen Watkins Harper

1825–1911 ◆ poet, writer, abolitionist, feminist, and lecturer
◆ a founding member of the National Association of Colored
Women ◆ proponent of women's suffrage ◆ "The Two Offers" is
the first short story credited to a black author ◆ best known for her
novel, *Iola Leroy*

While I am in favor of universal suffrage, yet I know that the colored man needs something more than a vote in his hand. . . . A man landless, ignorant, and poor may use the vote against his interests; but with intelligence and land he holds in his hand the basis of power and elements of strength.

Make me a grave where'er you will, in a lowly plain, or a lofty hill; make it among earth's humblest graves, but not in a land where men are slaves.

For she is a mother—her child is a slave—and she'll give him his freedom, or find him a grave!

They never burn a man in the South that they do not kindle a fire around my soul.

Could slavery exist long if it did not sit on a commercial throne?

Men who are deaf to the claims of mercy, and oblivious to the demands of justice, can feel when money is slipping from their pockets.

Justice is always uncompromising in its claims and inexorable in its demands. The laws of the universe are never repealed to accommodate our follies.

Our masters always tried to hide book learning from our eyes; knowledge didn't agree with slavery—'twould make us all too wise.

Mothers stood, with streaming eyes, and saw their dearest children sold, unheeded rose their bitter cries, while tyrants barter'd them for gold.

No nation can gain its full measure of enlightenment and happiness if one-half of it is free and the other half is fettered. China compressed the feet of her women and thereby retarded the steps of her men. The elements of a nation's weakness must ever be found at the hearthstone.

A government which can protect and defend its citizens from wrong and outrage and does not is vicious. A government which would do it and cannot is weak.

What is wrong in woman's life in man's cannot be right.

Dorothy Height

1912–2010 ◆ "Godmother of the Women's Movement"
◆ educator, feminist, and social activist ◆ founder and director of
the YWCA's Center for Racial Justice ◆ head of the National
Council of Negro Women ◆ key figure in the civil rights
movement of the sixties ◆ awarded a Congressional Gold Medal

We are not a problem people; we are a people with problems. We have historic strengths; we have survived because of family.

When you're a black woman, you seldom get to do what you just want to do; you always do what you have to do.

A Negro woman has the same kind of problems as other women, but she can't take the same things for granted.

Greatness is not measured by what a man or woman accomplishes, but by the opposition he or she has to overcome to reach his or her goals.

If you worry about who is going to get credit, you don't get much work done.

The major energies of black people in America historically have had to be directed to attaining the most elementary human freedoms (such as owning one's own body and the fruits thereof) that our white sisters and brothers take for granted.

Without community service, we would not have a strong quality of life. It's important to the person who serves as well as the recipient. It's the way in which we grow and develop.

With drugs and television and things of that sort, young people really have to work against being spectators rather than involved participants.

I want to be remembered as someone who used herself and anything she could touch to work for justice and freedom. . . . I want to be remembered as one who tried.

Jimi Hendrix

1942–1970 ◆ electric guitarist and singer-songwriter ◆
his Woodstock performance of the "Star-Spangled Banner" became
an instant classic and an anthem for the times ◆ Rock and Roll
Hall of Fame and recipient of the Grammy Awards
Lifetime Achievement Award

Knowledge speaks, but wisdom listens.

I've been imitated so well I've heard people copy my mistakes.

I sacrifice part of my soul every time I play.

I wish they'd had electric guitars in cotton fields back in the good old days. A whole lot of things would've been straightened out.

We call it "Electric Church Music" because to us music is a religion.

Blues is easy to play, but hard to feel.

Technically, I am not a guitar player, all I play is truth and emotion.

Imagination is the key to my lyrics. The rest is painted with a little science fiction.

Music is a safe kind of high.

The story of life is quicker than the blink of an eye, the story of love is hello, goodbye.

When the power of love overcomes the love of power, the world will know peace.

You have to give people something to dream on.

Anita Hill

Born 1956 ◆ lawyer, educator, writer, and feminist ◆ best known
for her testimony during the 1991 Senate confirmation hearings of
Supreme Court Justice nominee Clarence Thomas ◆ author of
Speaking Truth to Power

[*on Clarence Thomas*] Here is a person who is in charge of protecting rights of women and other groups in the workplace and he is using his position of power for personal gain . . . And he did it in a very ugly and intimidating way.

[*on her role in Clarence Thomas' confirmation hearings*] I resent the idea that people would blame the messenger for the message, rather than looking at the content of the message itself.

If you think about the way the hearings were structured, the hearings were really about Thomas' race and my gender.

My message is about changing our way of thinking about women and abuses of power.

Women who accuse men, particularly powerful men, of harassment, are often confronted with the reality of the men's sense that they are more important than women, as a group.

The invocation of cultural excuses for gender subordination and abuse is not only a distortion of community mores, it is a manipulative excuse for illegal behavior.

I think . . . as African-American women, we are always trained to value our community even at the expense of ourselves.

I think it would be irresponsible for me not to say what I really believe in my heart to be true—that there are some serious inequities that we face as women and that we can work to address these inequities.

Because I and my reality did not comport with what they accepted as their reality, I and my reality had to be reconstructed by the Senate committee members with assistance from the press and others.

I am really proud to be a part in whatever way of women becoming active in the political scene. I think it was the first time that people came to terms with the reality of what it meant to have a Senate made up of ninety-eight men and two women.

Chester Himes

1909–1984 ◆ writer best known for his detective fiction ◆ books
include *If He Hollers Let Him Go, Cotton Comes to Harlem,* and
his two volumes of autobiography, *The Quality of Hurt* and
My Life of Absurdity

Realism and absurdity are so similar in the lives of American blacks one cannot tell the difference.

[My] father was born and raised in the tradition of the Southern Uncle Tom; the tradition derived from the inherited slave mentality which accepts the premise that white people know best.

The American black is a new race of man; the only new race of man to come into being in modern times.

Man cannot live without some knowledge of the purpose of life. If he can find no purpose in life, he creates one in the inevitability of death.

American violence is public life, it's a public way of life, it became a form, a detective story form. So I should think that any number of black writers should go into the detective story form.

Martyrs are needed to create incidents. Incidents are needed to create revolutions. Revolutions are needed to create progress.

There can be only one (I repeat: *Only one*) aim of a revolution by Negro Americans: *That is the enforcement of the Constitution of the United States. . . . Therefore Negro Americans could not revolt for any other reason.* This is what a Negro American revolution will be: A revolution by a racial minority for the enforcement of the democratic laws already in existence.

Gregory Hines

1946–2003 ◆ stage, screen and TV actor, dancer, and
choreographer ◆ winner of a Tony award for *Jelly's Last Jam*
◆ films include *Cotton Club* and *White Nights* ◆ star of the
TV miniseries *Bojangles*

I don't remember not dancing. When I realized I was alive and these were my parents, and I could walk and talk, I could dance.

I never wanted to be a star, I just wanted to get work.

There were times when we were broke and I knew it. Dad found a way to sacrifice a quarter for me. I must keep that natural circle of love going around for my own son.

Remember, luck is opportunity meeting up with preparation, so you must prepare yourself to be lucky.

Eric Holder, Jr.

Born 1951 ◆ lawyer, judge, U.S. attorney (for the District of
Columbia), deputy attorney general ◆ first African-American
attorney general (the Obama administration)

In racial terms the country that existed before the civil rights struggle is almost unrecognizable to us today. Separate public facilities, separate entrances, poll taxes, legal discrimination, forced labor, in essence an American apartheid, all were part of an America that the movement destroyed.

Though this nation has proudly thought of itself as an ethnic melting pot, in things racial we have always been and continue to be, in too many ways, essentially a nation of cowards.

It is not safe for this nation to assume that the unaddressed social problems in the poorest parts of our country can be isolated and will not ultimately affect the larger society.

The civil rights movement made America, if not perfect, better. . . . [T]he other major social movements of the latter half of the twentieth century—feminism, the nation's treatment of other minority groups, even the anti-war effort, were all tied in some way to the spirit that was set free by the quest for African-American equality.

One cannot truly understand America without understanding the historical experience of black people in this nation. Simply put, to get to the heart of this country one must examine its racial soul.

Billie Holiday

1915–1959 ◆ "Lady Day" ◆ singer, lyricist, and song stylist
◆ seminal influence on jazz and pop singers ◆ best known songs
include "Gloomy Sunday," "Strange Fruit," and "God Bless
the Child" ◆ autobiography, *Lady Sings the Blues*

I'm always making a comeback but nobody ever tells me where I've been.

If you find a tune that's got something to do with you, you just feel it, and when you sing it, other people feel it, too.

Dope never helped anybody sing better or play music better or do anything better. All dope can do for you is kill you—and kill you the long, slow, hard way. And it can kill the people you love right along with you.

Sometimes it's worse to win a fight than to lose.

When you're poor, you grow up fast.

It is the easiest thing in the world to say every broad for herself— saying it and acting that way is one thing that's kept some of us behind the eight ball where we've been living for a hundred years.

You can be up to your boobies in white satin, with gardenias in your hair and no sugar cane for miles, but you can still be working on a plantation.

Somebody once said we never know what is enough until we know what's more than enough.

bell hooks

Born 1952 ✦ a.k.a. Gloria Jean Watkins ✦ poet, writer, educator,
feminist, and social activist ✦ books include *Talking Back:
Thinking Feminist, Thinking Black, Ain't I A Woman:
Black Women and Feminism,* and the children's book,
Happy to Be Nappy

I feel that part of my mission as an artist—this is what binds me
culturally to an Ice Cube and even a Snoop Doggy Dog—is understanding the beauty and aesthetic complexity in the vernacular.

For black people, the pain of learning that we cannot control our
images, how we see ourselves (if our vision is not decolonized), or
how we are seen is so intense that it rends us. It rips and tears at the
seams of our efforts to construct self and identity.

Black women resisted [white supremacist culture] by making homes
where all black people could strive to be subjects, not objects, where
we could be affirmed in our minds and hearts despite poverty, hardship,
and deprivation, where we could restore to ourselves the dignity denied
us on the outside in the public world.

Poetry was one literary expression that was absolutely respected in
our working-class household.

Secrets find a way out in sleep . . . It is the place where there is no
pretense.

Fundamentally the purpose of my knowing was so I could serve
those who did not know, so that I could learn and teach my own—
education as the practice of freedom.

Sexism has diminished the power of all black liberation struggles—
reformist or revolutionary.

Benjamin L. Hooks

1925–2010 ✦ orator, minister, judge, businessman, and civil rights
activist ✦ commissioner of the FCC ✦ executive director of the
NAACP ✦ autobiography, *The March of Civil Rights*

[*on segregated public facilities*] I wish I could tell you every time I
was on the highway and couldn't use a restroom. My bladder is
messed up because of that.

No longer can we provide polite, explicable reasons why Black America cannot do more for itself. I am calling for a moratorium on excuses. I challenge black America today all of us to set aside our alibis.

We've come a long way, but it's like nibbling at the edge of darkness.

It is a sad commentary on our times that blatant appeals to race still can divide us when so many urgent problems beset our nation.

Lena Horne

1917–2010 ◆ jazz singer, actress, dancer, TV personality, and civil rights activist ◆ one of the first African Americans to be signed to a long-term contract by a major Hollywood studio ◆ films include *Cabin in the Sky* and *Stormy Weather* ◆ Autobiography, *Lena*

Because time has been good to me, I treat it with great respect.

You have to be taught to be second class; you're not born that way.

It's an irony, but as true as anything in this world: when you're poor you need, in a deep, aching kind of way, luxuries. You need them, psychologically, as you never do when you're well off.

If patrons did not object to a Negro using the elevators or taking a shower or entertaining visitors in a suite, how could they object to her staying overnight? The contortions of logic which segregation forces on people would alone make it worthwhile to abandon.

It was a damn fight everywhere I was, every place I worked, in New York, in Hollywood, all over the world.

What an endless chain of unhappiness prejudice forges.

Music was, and perhaps still is, the area of my life where the question of color comes second and the question of whether you play good or not is the one you have to answer as a test of admission into society.

Marilyn Monroe and I discussed it often and agreed it would be nice if we could be strong enough in ourselves as women and not just there to make the male audience want to go to bed with us.

When "interested" people began to try to give me different "images" of myself, I came to realize that nobody (and certainly not yet myself) had any sound image to give a woman who stood between the two conventional ideas of Negro womanhood: the "good," quiet Negro woman who scrubbed and cooked and was a respectable servant—and the whore.

Over the years, I have not learned to love white people any more or less. . . . I just happen to feel more in my own skin with black people.

[at age eighty] My identity is very clear to me now. I am a black woman. I'm free. I no longer have to be a "credit." I don't have to be a symbol to anybody; I don't have to be a first to anybody. I don't have to be an imitation of a white woman that Hollywood sort of hoped I'd become. I'm me, and I'm like nobody else.

The whole thing that made me a star was the war [World War II]. Of course the black guys couldn't put Betty Grable's pictures in their footlockers. But they could put mine.

It's not the load that breaks you down. It's the way you carry it.

Langston Hughes

1902–1967 ◆ novelist, poet, and playwright ◆ Harlem Renaissance notable and poet laureate of Harlem ◆ books include *The Weary Blues, Not Without Laughter, Simple Speaks His Mind*, and his autobiography, *The Big Sea*

I have discovered in life that there are ways of getting almost anywhere you want to go, if you really want to go.

We Negro writers, just by being black, have been on the blacklist all our lives . . . Censorship for us begins at the color line.

This is the mountain standing in the way of any true Negro art in America—this urge to whiteness, the desire to pour racial individuality into the mold of American standardization, and to be as little Negro and as much American as possible.

Many of our institutions apparently are not trying to make men and women of their students at all. They are doing their best to produce spineless Uncle Toms, uninformed, and full of mental and moral evasions.

One of the most promising young Negro poets said to me once, "I want to be a poet—not a Negro poet," meaning, I believe, "I want to write like a white poet"; meaning subconsciously, "I would like to be a white poet"; meaning behind that, "I would like to be white." And I was sorry the young man said that, for no great poet has ever been afraid of being himself.

Jazz to me is one of the inherent expressions of Negro life in America; the eternal tom-tom beating in the Negro soul—the tom-tom of revolt against weariness in a white world, a world of subway trains, and work, work, work; the tom-tom of joy and laughter, and pain swallowed in a smile.

I was in love with Harlem long before I got there. . . . Had I been a rich young man, I would have bought a house in Harlem and built musical steps up to the front door, and installed chimes that at the press of a button played Ellington tunes.

Harlem was like a great magnet for the Negro intellectual, pulling him from everywhere.

Melting pot Harlem—Harlem of honey and chocolate and caramel and rum and vinegar and lemon and lime and gall. Dusky dream Harlem rumbling into a nightmare tunnel where the subway from the Bronx keeps right on downtown, where the money from the clubs goes right on back downtown, where the jazz is drained to Broadway.

Humor is laughing at what you haven't got when you ought to have it.

O, yes, I say it plain, America never was America to me, and yet I swear this oath—America will be!

We Negroes of America are tired of a world divided superficially on the basis of blood and color, but in reality on the basis of poverty and power—the rich over the poor, no matter what their color.

Life for me ain't been no crystal stair.

Alberta Hunter

1895–1984 ◆ blues singer-songwriter and nurse ◆ sang with such
jazz greats as Eubie Blake, Fats Waller, and Louis Armstrong
◆ starred on Broadway, toured in Europe ◆ subject of the film
documentary, *Alberta Hunter: My Castle's Rockin'*

Blues means what milk does to a baby. Blues is what the spirit is to
the minister. We sing the blues because our hearts have been hurt,
our souls have been disturbed.

The musicians that didn't know music could play the best blues. I
know that I don't want no musicians who know all about music
playin' for me.

Can't a man alive mistreat me, 'cause I know who I am.

Until they put that sand and dirt in my face I will not sit in church
all day.

Zora Neale Hurston

1891–1960 ◆ writer and anthropologist ◆ Harlem Renaissance
notable ◆ books include novels, short stories and essays, collections
of black folklore, as well as an autobiography,
Dust Tracks on a Road

I have the map of Dixie on my tongue.

It is hard to apply oneself to study when there is no money to pay for
food and lodging.

When a man keeps beating me to the draw mentally, he begins to
get glamorous.

It is easy to be hopeful in the day when you can see the things you
wish on.

I'll wrassle me up a future or die trying.

Fighting is a game where everyone is the loser.

Don't you know you can't git de best of no woman in the talkin'
game? Her tongue is all de weapon a woman got.

There are years that ask questions and years that answer.

I have been in Sorrow's kitchen and licked out all the pots.

When one is too old for love, one finds great comfort in good dinners.

His road of thought is what makes every man what he is.

Love makes your soul crawl out from its hiding place.

I had a way of life inside me and I wanted it with a want that was twisting me.

Nothing had been done in Negro folklore when the greatest cultural wealth of the continent was disappearing without the world ever realizing it had ever been.

Belief in magic is older than writing.

Roll your eyes in ecstasy and ape his every move, but until we have placed something upon his street corner that is our own, we are right back where we were when they filed our iron collar off.

There is something about poverty that smells like death. Dead dreams dropping off the heart like leaves in a dry season and rotting around the feet; impulses smothered too long in the fetid air of underground caves. The soul lives in a sickly air. People can be slave-ships in shoes.

I am not tragically colored. There is no great sorrow dammed up in my soul, nor lurking behind my eyes. I do not mind at all. . . . No, I do not weep at the world—I am too busy sharpening my oyster knife.

I have come to know by experience that work is the nearest thing to happiness that I can find.

Sometimes I feel discriminated against, but it docs not makc mc angry. It merely astonishes me. How can anyone deny themselves the pleasure of my company?

Jesse Jackson

Born 1941 ◆ minister, presidential candidate, and civil rights leader
◆ close associate of Martin Luther King ◆ founder of PUSH
(People United to Save Humanity)

We must turn *to* each other and not *on* each other.

Time is neutral and does not change things. With courage and initiative, leaders change things.

The only justification for ever looking down on somebody is to pick them up.

The only protection against genocide is to remain necessary.

If you run [for office], you might lose. If you don't run, you're guaranteed to lose.

If you raise up truth, it's magnetic. It has a way of drawing people.

Your children need your presence more than your presents.

With no sense of history, you exist in a vacuum. How can you appreciate Mike Tyson without understanding the significance of Joe Louis? How can you applaud Michael Jackson and not realize he stands on the shoulders of Sammy Davis, Jr.? Could there be a David Dinkins without an Adam Clayton Powell?

The reason Joe Louis will always be respected in the black community is that at a time when other blacks couldn't even talk back to white people, Joe Louis was beating them up, knocking them down and making them bleed.

We are far more threatened by the dope than the rope . . . We lose more lives annually to the crime of blacks killing blacks than the sum total of lynchings in the entire history of the country.

We are not a perfect people. Yet, we are called to a perfect mission; our mission, to feed the hungry, to clothe the naked, to house the homeless, to teach the illiterate, to provide jobs for the jobless, and to choose the human race over the nuclear race.

Both tears and sweat are salty, but they render a different result. Tears will get you sympathy; sweat will get you change.

The burden of being black is that you have to be superior just to be equal. But the glory of it is that, once you achieve, you have achieved indeed.

My constituency is the damned, disinherited, disrespected, and the despised.

I just want to take common sense to high places.

Mahalia Jackson

1911–1972 ◆ "Queen of Gospel" ◆ singer of gospel, blues,
hymns, and spirituals, and civil rights activist ◆ autobiography,
Movin' on Up

Singing the old spirituals for blacks who are not ashamed of being black or from the South helps me fight for my people.

Anybody that sings the blues is in a deep pit, yelling for help.

Blues are the songs of despair, but gospel songs are the songs of hope.

Without a song, each day would be a century.

It's easy to be independent when you've got money. But to be independent when you haven't got a thing, that's the Lord's test.

Black promoters oppressed me before white promoters ever got hold of me. Don't talk skin to me.

No one can hurt the gospel because the gospel is strong, like a two-headed sword is strong.

Faith and prayer are the vitamins of the soul; man cannot live in health without them.

The old Devil gets mad when you're trying to do good. Pray that God will move the stumbling blocks.

Until my singing made me famous, I'd lived so far inside the colored people's world that I didn't have to pay attention every day to the way some white people in this country act toward a person with a darker skin.

[about the time restrictions imposed on her TV appearances] Time is important to me because I want to sing loud enough to leave a message. I'm used to singing in churches where nobody would dare stop me until the Lord arrives!

Michael Jackson

1958–2009 ♦ "King of Pop" ♦ singer-songwriter, dancer,
choreographer, and actor ♦ career began at the age of five with his
family's group, the Jackson Five ♦ his megahit *Thriller* is one of the
bestselling albums of all time ♦ autobiography, *Moonwalk*

The greatest education in the world is watching the masters at
work.

I happen to be color blind. I don't hire color. I hire competence.

I'm never pleased with anything, I'm a perfectionist.

If all the people in Hollywood who have had plastic surgery . . . went
on vacation, there wouldn't be a person left in town.

I wake up from dreams and go "Wow, put this down on paper." . . .
That's why I hate to take credit for the songs I've written. I feel that
somewhere, someplace, it's been done and I'm just a courier
bringing it out into the world.

I hate it when I meet fans and they try and tear bits of my hair and
clothing. It's like they're trying to tear your soul away.

The same music governs the rhythm of the seasons, the pulse of our
heartbeats, the migration of the birds, the ebb and flow of ocean
tides, the cycles of growth, evolution and dissolution. It's music, it's
rhythm.

Nothing can harm me when I'm on stage—nothing. That's really
me. That's what I'm here to do. I'm totally at home on stage. That's
where I live. That's where I was born. That's where I'm safe.

Reggie Jackson

Born 1946 ♦ known as "Mr. October" for his steady excellence in
play-off and World Series games ♦ placed in the top ten of all-time
home-run hitters with 563 home runs ♦ Baseball Hall of Fame
♦ autobiography, *Reggie*

[on his popularity] I could put meat in the seats.

Climb the ladder of equality with dignity.

I don't mind getting beaten, but I hate to lose.

I wasn't exactly brought up in one of those Norman Rockwell paintings you used to see on the cover of the *Saturday Evening Post*.

In the building I live in on Park Avenue there are ten people who could buy the Yankees, but none of them could hit the ball out of Yankee stadium.

Please God, let me hit one. I'll tell everybody you did it.

The greatest manager has a knack for making ballplayers think they are better than they think they are.

I feel that the most important requirement in success is learning to overcome failure. You must learn to tolerate it, but never accept it.

Fans don't boo nobodies.

Money lets you live better. It doesn't make you play better.

When I was a boy, I was "colored." As a teenager, I was a "Negro." As a young man, I was "black." As an older man, I was "African-American." Now that I'm an old man, I'm "multi-cultural."

Harriet Ann Jacobs

c. 1813–1897 ◆ abolitionist, social reformer, and slave narrator
◆ spent seven years hidden in a cramped attic space to escape
detection as a fugitive slave ◆ autobiography, *Incidents in
the Life of a Slave Girl*

Slaveholders have been cunning enough to enact that "the child shall follow the condition of the *mother*," not of the *father*; thus taking care that licentiousness shall not interfere with avarice.

I was twenty-one years in that cage of obscene birds. I can testify, from my own experience and observation, that slavery is a curse to the whites as well as to the blacks.

You never knew what it is to be a slave; to be entirely unprotected by law or custom; to have the laws reduce you to the condition of a chattel, entirely subject to the will of another. You never exhausted your ingenuity in avoiding the snares, and eluding the power of a hated tyrant; you never shuddered at the sound of his footsteps, and trembled within hearing of his voice.

We all know that the memory of a faithful slave does not avail much to save her children from the auction block.

Slavery is terrible for men; but it is far more terrible for women. . . . If God has bestowed beauty upon her, it will prove her greatest curse. That which commands admiration in the white woman only hastens the degradation of the female slave.

My master had power and law on his side; I had a determined will. There is might in each.

There are no bonds so strong as those which are formed by suffering together.

So I was *sold* at last! A human being *sold* in the free city of New York! The bill of sale is on record, and future generations will learn from it that women were articles of traffic in New York, late in the nineteenth century of the Christian religion.

Friend! It is a common word, often lightly used. Like other good and beautiful things, it may be tarnished by careless handling.

There are wrongs that even the grave does not bury.

Judith Jamison

Born 1943 ◆ dancer and choreographer ◆ artistic director of the
Alvin Ailey American Dance Theater ◆ performed on Broadway in
Sophisticated Ladies ◆ autobiography, *Dancing Spirit*

Excellence is the name of the game no matter what color or what country you're from.

People come to see beauty, and I dance to give it to them.

While [the Alvin Ailey American Dance Theater is] here to celebrate the black experience, we're not here to be exclusionary about who can do that with us. Being inclusive is part of our African tradition.

Once you've danced, you always dance. You can't deny the gifts that God sends your way.

Dance is bigger than the physical body. When you extend your arm, it doesn't stop at the end of your fingers, because you're dancing bigger than that; you're dancing spirit.

So many people dwell on negativity and I've survived by ignoring it: it dims your light and it's harder each time to turn the power up again.

Charles R. Johnson

Born 1948 ✦ writer, screenwriter, cartoonist, and
educator ✦ winner of the National Book Award for
Middle Passage ✦ other books include *Oxherding Tale, Dreamer,*
and *Turning the Wheel*

Our experience as black men and women completely outstrips our
perception—black life is ambiguous, and a kaleidoscope of meanings,
rich, multi-sided . . . [W]e have frozen our vision in figures that
caricature, at best, the complexity of our lives and leave the real
artistic chore of interpretation unfinished.

The built-in danger of . . . cultural nationalism is the very tendency
toward provincialism, separatism, and essential modes of thought
that characterize the Anglophilia it opposes.

[Black fiction will become one of] increasing intellectual and
artistic generosity, one that enables us as a people, as a culture, to
move from narrow complaint to broad celebration.

In a dangerous world, a realm of disasters, a place of grief and pain,
a sensible man made *himself* dangerous, more frightening than all
the social and political "accidents" that might befall him. He was, in
a way, a specialist in survival.

Wealth isn't what a man has, but what he is.

Writing itself is the best teacher of writing, so a young or old writer
must learn that, if necessary, his ratio of throwaway to keep pages
might turn out to be twenty to one.

I found my way to make my peace with the recent past by turning it
into WORD.

Earvin "Magic" Johnson

Born 1959 ✦ basketball player and motivational speaker
✦ Basketball Hall of Fame ✦ founder of the Magic Johnson
Foundation for AIDS research ✦ autobiography, *My Life*

If people around you aren't going anywhere, if their dreams are no
bigger than hanging out on the corner, or if they're dragging you
down, get rid of them. Negative people can sap your energy so fast,
and they can take your dreams from you, too.

All kids need is a little help, a little hope, and somebody who believes in them.

When you face a crisis, you know who your true friends are.

You're the only one who can make the difference. Whatever your dream is, go for it.

Magic is who I am on the basketball court. Earvin is who I am.

Jack Johnson

1878–1946 ◆ world's first African-American heavyweight boxer and first black sports icon ◆ autobiographical works, *Jack Johnson: In the Ring and Out* and *My Life and Battles*

For every point I'm given, I'll have earned two, because I'm a Negro.

[quipped to Tommy Burns, from whom he won the heavyweight crown] Who told you I was yellow? You're white, Tommy—white as the flag of surrender!

[on winning the heavyweight crown] To me it was not a racial triumph, but there were those who were to take this view of the situation, and almost immediately a great hue and cry went up because a colored man was holding the championship.

I made a lot of mistakes out of the ring, but I never made any in it.

Don't let your dreams be dreams.

James Weldon Johnson

1871–1938 ◆ poet, writer, songwriter, educator, and civil rights activist ◆ co-wrote "Lift Every Voice and Sing," the Negro National Anthem ◆ books include *Black Manhattan* and *God's Trombones: Seven Negro Sermons in Verse*, and his autobiography, *Along This Way*

Every race and every nation should be judged by the best it has been able to produce, not by the worst.

The fact is, nothing great or enduring, especially in music, has ever sprung full-fledged and unprecedented from the brain of any master; the best he gives to the world he gathers from the hearts of the people, and runs it through the alembic of his genius.

From the day I set foot in France, I became aware of the working of a miracle within me. . . . I recaptured for the first time since childhood the sense of being just a human being.

A good part of white America frequently asks the question, "What shall we do with the Negro?" In asking the question it completely ignores the fact that the Negro is doing something with himself, and also the equally important fact that the Negro all the while is doing something with America.

It is from the blues that all that may be called American music derives its most distinctive characteristic.

The influence which the Negro has exercised on the art of dancing in this country has been almost absolute.

Harlem [is] . . . a place where life wakes up at night.

You are young, gifted, and black. We must begin to tell our young, there's a world waiting for you, yours is the quest that's just begun.

My inner life is mine, and I shall defend and maintain its integrity against all the powers of hell.

New York is the most fatally fascinating thing in America.

In the core of the heart of the American race problem the sex factor is rooted; rooted so deeply that it is not always recognized when it shows on the surface.

Though the black man fights passively, he nevertheless fights; and his passive resistance is more effective at present than active resistance could possibly be. He bears the fury of the storm as does the willow tree.

I lived to learn that in the world of sport all men win alike, but lose differently; and so gamblers are rated, not by the way in which they win, but by the way in which they lose.

Evil is a force, and, like the physical and chemical forces, one cannot annihilate it; we may only change its form.

Labor is the fabled magician's wand, the philosophers' stone, and the cap of good fortune.

I had made up my mind that since I was not going to be a Negro, I would avail myself of every possible opportunity to make a white man's success; and that, if it can be summed up in any one word, means "money."

The stereotype is that the Negro is nothing more than a beggar at the gate of the nation, waiting to be thrown crumbs of civilization. Through his artistic efforts the Negro is smashing this immemorial stereotype faster than he has ever done through any other method he has been able to use.

Young man, young man, your arm's too short to box with God.

I have been amazed and amused watching white people dancing to a Negro band in a Harlem cabaret; attempting to throw off the crusts and layers of inhibitions laid on by sophisticated civilizations . . . trying to work their way back into that jungle which was the original Garden of Eden; in a word, doing their best to pass for colored.

John H. Johnson

1918–2005 ◆ publisher and entrepreneur ◆ founder of the Johnson Publishing Company, publisher of *Jet* and *Ebony* magazines, among others ◆ the first African American to appear on the Forbes 400 list ◆ autobiography, *Succeeding Against the Odds*

Never before have so many white Americans paid black Americans that sincerest form of flattery—imitation.

To succeed, one must be creative and persistent.

If you can somehow think and dream of success in small steps, every time you make a step, every time you accomplish a small goal, it gives you confidence to go on from there.

Every day I run scared. That's the only way I can stay ahead.

It's better to get smart than to get mad. I try not to get so insulted that I will not take advantage of an opportunity to persuade people to change their minds.

I made some of my luck. I made it by working hard and trusting the logic of events, which always favor the bold and the active and the prepared.

James Earl Jones

Born 1931 ◆ actor of stage and screen, and voiceover artist ◆ plays
include *The Great White Hope* and *Othello* ◆ films include
Field of Dreams and *Cry, the Beloved Country* ◆ the voice of
Darth Vader in the original *Star Wars* trilogy ◆ memoirs,
James Earl Jones and *Voices and Silences*

One of the hardest things in life is having words in your heart that
you can't utter.

When I read great literature, great drama, speeches, or sermons,
I feel that the human mind has not achieved anything greater
than the ability to share feelings and thoughts through
language.

Your own need to be shines out of any dream or creation you imagine.

Once you begin to explain or excuse all events on racial grounds,
you begin to indulge in the perilous mythology of race. It is
dangerous to say "The white man is the cause of my problems" or
"The black man is the cause of my problems." Substitute any
color—the danger is implicit.

Out in the country, with few books or strangers, and no such thing as
television, we depended on the stories we knew, and the stories we
could invent and tell ourselves. I grew up with the spoken word.

Quincy Jones

Born 1933 ◆ musician, composer, arranger, producer, and
entrepreneur ◆ founder of Qwest Records and *Vibe* magazine
◆ producer of Michael Jackson's bestselling album *Thriller*
◆ winner of the Grammy Legend Award ◆ autobiography, *Q*

In the thirties and early forties, we had no role models. Think of it.
There was no TV. The only black on radio was Rochester. Even
Amos and Andy were white. In sports, there was Joe Louis. How can
anybody grow up and aspire to something if it doesn't exist?

It's amazing how much trouble you can get in when you don't have
anything else to do.

The most deadly thing about cocaine is that it separates you from
your soul.

You have to know that your real home is within.

Imagine what a harmonious world it could be if every single person, both young and old, shared a little of what he is good at doing.

I had a good ear, so I realized that printed music was just about reminding you what to play.

You get a little band together, and then you get a few jobs. You take four guys that sound half bad, but if they're twenty-five percent each, they can give 100%, you know?

All my life I've had this almost criminal optimism. I didn't care what happened, the glass was always going to be half full.

Barbara Jordan

1936–1996 ◆ attorney, legislator, and educator ◆ the first
African-American woman from the South elected to the U.S. House
of Representatives ◆ member of the House Judiciary Committee
during Richard M. Nixon's impeachment hearings
◆ autobiography, *Barbara Jordan: A Self-Portrait*

I felt somehow for many years that George Washington and Alexander Hamilton just left me out [of the Constitution] by mistake. But through the process of amendment, interpretation, and court decision, I have finally been included in "We, the people."

Education remains the key to both economic and political empowerment.

Do not call for black power or green power. Call for brain power.

In Congress, one chips away, one does not make bold strokes. After six years I had wearied of the little chips that I could put on a woodpile.

Most Negroes have a little black militancy swimming around in them and most white people have a little Ku Klux Klan swimming around in them. If we'd be honest with each other, we would discover we are all victims of the racism that is historically part of this country.

What the people want is very simple. They want an America as good as its promise.

June Jordan

1936–2002 ◆ poet, writer, educator, feminist, and civil rights
activist ◆ her numerous books span many genres including works
for children and young adults ◆ titles include *His Own Where,
Naming Our Own Destiny: New and Selected Poems*, and
Towards Home: Political Essays

As a black woman/feminist, I must look about me, with trembling, and with shocked anger, at the endless waste, the endless suffocation of my sisters. . . . How is my own lifework serving to end these tyrannies, these corrosions of sacred possibility?

Language is political. That's why you and me, my Brother and Sister, that's why we supposed to choke our natural self into the weird, lying, barbarous, unreal, white speech and writing habits that the schools lay down like holy law.

We have been flexible, ingenious, and innovative or we have perished. And we have not perished.

There are two ways to worry words. One is hoping for the greatest possible beauty in what is created. The other is to tell the truth.

My own momma done better than she could and my momma's momma, *she* done better than I could. And *everybody's momma* done better than anybody had any right to expect she would.

We do not deride the fears of prospering white America. A nation of violence and private property has every reason to dread the violated and the deprived.

There is difference, and there is power. And who holds the power shall decide the meaning of difference.

Poetry is a political act because it involves telling the truth.

Behold my heart of darkness as it quickens now, with rage!

Michael Jordan

Born 1963 ◆ "Air Jordan" ◆ basketball player and sports icon
◆ five-time winner of the NBA's MVP award ◆ memoirs,
For the Love of the Game: My Story and *Driven from Within*

Because I want every kid to be viewed as a person rather than as a member of a certain race does not mean that I'm not black enough. . . . Do they want me to be positive just for black kids and negative for everybody else?

You have to expect things of yourself before you can do them.

I have missed more than 9,000 shots in my career. I have lost almost 300 games. On twenty-six occasions I have been entrusted to take the game-winning shot . . . and missed. And I have failed over and over and over again in my life. And that is why I succeed.

I know fear is an obstacle for some people, but it is an illusion to me. . . . Failure always made me try harder the next time.

If you run into a wall, don't turn around and give up. Figure out how to climb it, go through it, or work around it.

Talent wins games, but teamwork and intelligence win championships.

Jackie Joyner-Kersee

Born 1962 ◆ Olympic heptathlete, sports icon, and philanthropist
◆ winner of more Olympic medals than any other woman in track
and field events ◆ voted the Greatest Female Athlete of the
Twentieth Century by *Sports Illustrated for Women*
◆ autobiography, *A Kind of Grace*

It's better to look ahead and prepare than to look back and regret.

I always had something to shoot for each year: to jump one inch farther.

My grandma named me after Jacqueline Kennedy, hoping that someday I'd be the first lady of something.

I think it's the mark of a great player to be confident in tough situations.

The glory of sport comes from dedication, determination and desire.

Age is no barrier. It's a limitation you put on your mind.

I don't think being an athlete is unfeminine. I think of it as a kind of grace.

Florynce R. Kennedy

1916–2000 ✦ attorney, pro-abortion advocate, civil rights activist, and feminist ✦ represented the estates of Billie Holiday and Charlie Parker ✦ autobiography, *Color Me Flo: My Hard Life and Good Times*

If men could become pregnant, abortion would be a sacrament.

Our parents had us so convinced we were precious that by the time I found out I was nothing, it was already too late—I knew I was something.

Don't agonize, organize.

The biggest sin is sitting on your ass.

John Oliver Killens

1916–1987 ✦ novelist, educator, and social activist ✦ co-founder of the Harlem Writers Guild and founder of the National Black Writers Conference at Medgar Evers College ✦ books include *And Then We Heard the Thunder* and *The Cotillion: or, One Good Bull Is Half the Herd*

Western man wrote "his" history as if it were the history of the entire human race.

The Negro was invented in America.

Integration begins the day after the minds of the people are desegregated.

Who in the hell ever heard of a second-class citizen until they were invented in the United States? A person is either a citizen or he is not a citizen. You are either free or you are a slave.

Harlem is the largest plantation in this country.

A child must have a sense of selfhood, a knowledge that he is not here by sufferance, that his forebears contributed to the country and to the world.

The white man's juju is powerful stuff, but it cannot wish the Negro into invisibility.

Jamaica Kincaid

Born 1949 ◆ poet, writer, and educator ◆ screenwriter for the
documentary, *Life and Debt* ◆ books include *At the Bottom
of the River, Lucy*, and *The Autobiography of My Mother*

Already her mouth was turned down permanently at the corners,
as if to show that she had been born realizing that nobody else
behaved properly, and as if also she had been born knowing that
everything in life was a disappointment and her face was all set to
meet it.

What you want to defeat is the idea that says your individuality
doesn't count—that all you are is black. You want to say, "But I'm a
person. Not a political entity."

Black people don't like unhappy endings. Perhaps we have too
many.

Lying is the beginning of fiction. It was the beginning of my writing
life.

On their way to freedom, some people find riches, some people find
death.

Writing is really such an expression of personal growth. I don't know
how else to live. For me it is a matter of saving my life. I don't know
what I would do if I didn't write. It is a matter of living in the deepest
way.

B. B. King

Born 1925 ◆ "King of the Blues" ◆ blues guitarist, singer-
songwriter, and philanthropist ◆ hits include "The Thrill Is Gone"
◆ autobiography, *Blues All Around Me*

To be a black person and sing the blues, you are black twice.

[on musical styles] I don't think anybody steals anything; all of us
borrow.

Being an influence makes me happy, and keeps me on my toes
too. . . . [S]ome bluesmen are right where they were ten or twelve
years ago, like a petrified forest. I like to keep improving and
perfecting my way of playing so that every time I go on stage there's
something different about the way I play.

I guess the earliest sound of blues that I can remember was in the fields while people would be pickin' cotton or choppin' or somethin'. When I sing and play now I can hear those same sounds that I used to hear then as a kid.

Jazz is the big brother of the blues. If a guy's playing blues like we play, he's in high school. When he starts playing jazz it's like going on to college, to a school of higher learning.

My father was born on the plantation, I was born on the plantation. I wanted more for my children. This—the guitar—was my way out.

Maybe our forefathers couldn't keep their language together when they were taken from Africa, but this, the blues, was a language we invented to let people know we had something to say.

Coretta Scott King

1927–2006 ◆ civil rights advocate, social activist, feminist, and educator ◆ memoir, *My Life with Martin Luther King, Jr.*

There is a spirit and a need and a man at the beginning of every great human advance. Each of these must be right for that particular moment of history, or nothing happens.

Women, if the soul of the nation is to be saved, I believe that you must become its soul.

Homophobia is like racism and anti-Semitism and other forms of bigotry in that it seeks to dehumanize a large group of people, to deny their humanity, their dignity and personhood.

Hate is too great a burden to bear. It injures the hater more than it injures the hated.

Martin Luther King, Jr.

1929–1968 ◆ civil rights leader, minister, writer, and orator
◆ winner of the Nobel Peace Prize ◆ books include *Stride Toward Freedom: The Montgomery Story, Why We Can't Wait*, and *The Autobiography of Martin Luther King, Jr.*

I have a dream that one day, on the red hills of Georgia, sons of former slaves and the sons of former slave-owners will be able to sit down together at the table of brotherhood. . . . I have a dream my four little children will one day live in a nation where they will not be judged by the color of their skin but by the content of their character.

When we allow freedom to ring, when we let it ring from every village and hamlet, from every state and city, we will be able to speed up that day when all of God's children—black men and white men, Jews and Gentiles, Catholics and Protestants—will be able to join hands and sing in the words of the old Negro spiritual, "Free at last, free at last; thank God Almighty, we are free at last."

Yes, I'm personally the victim of deferred dreams, of blasted hopes, but in spite of that I close today by saying I still have a dream, because, you know, you can't give up in life. If you lose hope, somehow you lose that vitality that keeps life moving, you lose the courage to be, and the quality that helps you go on in spite of all. And so today I still have a dream.

We can never be satisfied as long as a Negro in Mississippi cannot vote and a Negro in New York believes he has nothing for which to vote.

If America's soul becomes totally poisoned, part of the autopsy must read "Vietnam." It can never be saved so long as it destroys the deepest hopes of men the world over.

Injustice anywhere is a threat to justice everywhere.

We are inevitably our brother's keeper because we are our brother's brother.

Christianity has always insisted that the cross we bear precedes the crown we wear.

You can't reach good ends through evil means, because the means represent the seed and the end represents the tree.

The old law of an eye for an eye leaves everybody blind.

I submit that an individual who breaks a law that conscience tells him is unjust, and willingly accepts the penalty by staying in jail to arouse the conscience of the community over its injustice, is in reality expressing the very highest respect for the law.

A man who won't die for something is not fit to live.

To expect God to do everything while we do nothing is not faith but superstition.

Man is neither villain nor hero; he is rather both villain and hero.

There is nothing more dangerous than to build a society with a large segment of people in that society who feel that they have no stake in it; who feel that they have nothing to lose. People who have a stake in their society, protect that society, but when they don't have it, they unconsciously want to destroy it.

If a man is called to be a streetsweeper, he should sweep streets as Michelangelo painted, or Beethoven composed music, or Shakespeare wrote poetry. He should sweep streets so well that all the hosts of heaven and earth will pause to say, here lived a great streetsweeper who did his job well.

[Violence] is immoral because it is seeks to humiliate the opponent rather than win his understanding; it seeks to annihilate rather than to convert. Violence is immoral because it thrives on hatred rather than love.

Racism is a contempt for life, an arrogant assertion that one race is the center of value and object of devotion, before which other races must kneel in submission.

If physical death is the price that I must pay to free my white brothers and sisters from a permanent death of the spirit, then nothing can be more redemptive.

A genuine leader is not a searcher for consensus but a molder of consensus.

A man can't ride your back unless it's bent.

A nation that continues year after year to spend more money on military defense than on programs of social uplift is approaching spiritual doom.

Discrimination is a hellhound that gnaws at Negroes in every waking moment of their lives to remind them that the lie of their inferiority is accepted as truth in the society dominating them.

A right delayed is a right denied.

A riot is at bottom the language of the unheard.

Everybody can be great, because anybody can serve. You don't have to have a college degree to serve. You don't have to make your subject and verb agree to serve. You only need a heart full of grace. A soul generated by love.

Our lives begin to end the day we become silent about things that matter.

Faith is taking the first step even when you don't see the whole staircase.

Freedom is never voluntarily given by the oppressor; it must be demanded by the oppressed.

If we are wrong—the Supreme Court of this nation is wrong. If we are wrong—God Almighty is wrong! If we are wrong—Jesus of Nazareth was merely a utopian dreamer and never came down to earth! If we are wrong—justice is a lie!

Morals cannot be legislated, but behavior can be regulated. The law cannot make an employer love me, but it can keep him from refusing to hire me because of the color of my skin.

A good many observers have remarked that if equality could come at once, the Negro would not be ready for it. I submit that the white American is even more unprepared.

No one has ever heard the Jews publicly chant a slogan of Jewish power, but they have power. Through group identity, determination, and creative endeavor, they have gained it. . . . This is exactly what we must do.

The Western arrogance of feeling that it has everything to teach others and nothing to learn from them is not just.

True compassion is more than flinging a coin to a beggar; it is not haphazard and superficial. It comes to see that an edifice which produces beggars needs restructuring.

Truth pressed to earth will rise again . . . no lie can live forever.

Non-violence is a powerful and just weapon. It is a weapon unique in history, which cuts without wounding and ennobles the man who wields it. It is a sword that heals.

We must all learn to live together as Brothers. Or we will all perish together as fools.

If you find me sprawled out dead, I do not want you to retaliate with a single act of violence. I urge you to continue protesting with the same dignity and discipline you have shown so far.

Nella Larsen

1891–1964 ◆ writer, librarian, and nurse ◆ Harlem Renaissance
notable ◆ novels, *Quicksand* and *Passing* ◆ the first African-
American woman to be awarded a Guggenheim Fellowship

These people yapped loudly of race, of race consciousness, of race
pride, and yet suppressed its most delightful manifestations, love of
color, joy of rhythmic motion, naïve, spontaneous laughter, harmony,
radiance, and simplicity, all the essentials of spiritual beauty in the
race they had marked for destruction.

My old man died in a fine big house. My ma died in a shack. I
wonder where I'm gonna die, being neither white nor black?

Lies, injustice, and hypocrisy are a part of every ordinary community. Most people achieve a sort of protective immunity, a kind of
callousness, toward them. If they didn't, they couldn't endure.

What are friends for, if not to help bear our sins?

If a man calls me a nigger it's his fault the first time, but mine if he
has the opportunity to do it again.

It was . . . enough to suffer as a woman, an individual, on one's own
account, without having to suffer for the race as well. It was a
brutality, and undeserved.

Lead Belly

c. 1888–1949 ◆ a.k.a. Huddie William Ledbetter ◆ "King of the
Twelve-string Guitar" ◆ singer-songwriter and musician ◆ blues
icon ◆ classics include "Goodnight, Irene," "The Midnight
Special," and "Nobody Knows the Trouble I've Seen"

I'm just doing stuff. Letting the people know what American folk
music is, unwritten music, made up by the people.

I'll fight Jim Crow any place, any time. . . . One of the songs I'm
gonna sing is "We all in the same boat, brother. You rock it too far
to the right you fall in the waddah, rock it too far to the left you fall
in the same waddah, and it's just as wet on both sides."

If a white woman says something, it must be so, and she can say
something about a colored person, if it's a thousand colored men,
they kill all of 'em just for that one woman. If she ain't telling the

truth, it don't make any difference. Why? 'Cause it's Jim Crow, and I know it's so 'cause the Scottsboro boys can tell you about it.

The blues is like this. You lay down some night and you turn from one side of the bed to the other: all night long. It's not too cold in that bed, and it ain't too hot. But what's the matter? The blues has got you.

One thing, folks, you should all realize, six foot of dirt makes us all one size, for God made us all, and in Him we trust, nobody in this world is better than us.

Spike Lee

Born 1957 ◆ film director, producer, writer, actor, and social activist ◆ films include *She's Gotta Have It, Do the Right Thing, Malcolm X*, and *Clockers*

Film is not to be played with. It may be our most powerful medium and should be treated as such.

We've got to turn this backward thinking around where ignorance is championed over intelligence. Young black kids being ridiculed by their peers for getting A's and speaking proper English: that's criminal.

I think we've done more to hold ourselves back than anybody. If anybody's seen all my films, I put most of the blame on our shoulders and say, "Look, we're gonna have to do for ourselves."

America's the most violent country in the history of the world, that's just the way it is.

To me, the most important thing is to be truthful.

Without money, you have no control. Without control, you have no power.

Sex and racism have always been tied together. Look at the thousands of black men who got lynched and castrated. The reason the Klan came into being was to protect white southern women.

I think it is very important that films make people look at what they've forgotten.

People who have faults are a lot more interesting than people who are perfect.

Do the Right Thing.

Sugar Ray Leonard

Born 1956 ◆ boxer, broadcaster, inspirational speaker, fundraiser, and philanthropist ◆ winner of several world championship titles and an Olympic gold medal ◆ International Boxing Hall of Fame ◆ autobiography, *Sugar Ray*

We're all endowed with God-given talents. Mine happens to be hitting people in the head.

A fighter never knows when it's the last bell.

Boxing was not something I truly enjoyed. Like a lot of things in life, when you put the gloves on, it's better to give than to receive.

The only way for a fighter to get back in shape is to fight his way back.

Julius Lester

Born 1939 ◆ poet, writer, historian, folklorist, musician, educator, photographer, radio and TV personality, and civil rights activist ◆ books include *The Knee-High Man and Other Tales*, *And All Our Wounds Forgiven*, and his memoir, *Lovesong: Becoming a Jew*

One of my attributes is blackness, but that is not the sum total of my existence, and I refuse to allow society to make it so.

Perhaps one of the writer's tasks is to weave himself into others' pain.

[I knew] that the segregated world in which I was forced to live bounded by the white heat of hatred was not the only reality. Somewhere beyond that world, somewhere my eyes could not then penetrate, were dreams and possibilities, and I knew that this was true because the books I read ravenously, desperately, were voices from that world.

Often, the human animal dresses terror in rage, and expresses both in a way unlike either.

Being a failure at living your own life as best you can is better than being a success living the life somebody else says you should live.

To give good hugs you need to have some soft places.

John R. Lewis

Born 1940 ◆ politician and civil rights leader ◆ Congressman from Georgia ◆ participated in the Freedom Rides through the South, and the Selma to Montgomery marches, as well as the march on Washington for Jobs and Freedom (1963) ◆ memoir, *Walking with the Wind: A Memoir of the Movement*

The next time we march, we won't march on Washington, but we will march through the South, through the Heart of Dixie, the way Sherman did. We will make the action of the past few months look petty. And I say to you, WAKE UP, AMERICA!

We may not have chosen the time, but the time has chosen us.

War does not end strife—it sows it. War does not end hatred—it feeds it.

Alain Locke

1885–1954 ◆ "Father of the Harlem Renaissance" ◆ the first African-American Rhodes Scholar ◆ books include *Race Contacts and Interracial Relations: Lectures on the Theory and Practice of Race* and *The New Negro: An Interpretation*

Harlem is the precious fruit in the Garden of Eden, the big apple.

The position of the Negro in American culture is indeed a paradox. It almost passes understanding how and why a group of people can be socially despised, yet at the same time artistically esteemed and culturally influential, can be both an oppressed minority and a dominant cultural force.

Our poets have now stopped speaking for the Negro—they speak as Negroes.

[on Negro spirituals] Through their untarnishable beauty, they seem assured of the immortality of those great folk expressions that survive not so much through being typical of a group or representative of a period as by virtue of being fundamentally and everlastingly human.

Subtly, the conditions that are molding a New Negro are molding a new American attitude.

Africa is not only our mother, but in the light of most recent science is beginning to appear as the mother of civilization.

We must never forget that dance is the cradle of Negro music.

For generations in the mind of America, the Negro has been more of a formula than a human being—a something to be argued about, condemned or defended, to be "kept down," or "in his place," or "helped up," to be worried with or worried over, harassed or patronized, a social bogey or a social burden.

Art must discover and reveal the beauty which prejudice and caricature have overlaid.

It is a curious but inevitable irony that the American temperament, so notorious for its overweening confidence and self-esteem, should be of all temperaments least reflective, and for all its self-consciousness, should know itself so ill.

As with the Jew, persecution is making the Negro international.

The South has unconsciously absorbed the gift of [the Negro's] folk-temperament. In less than half a generation it will be easier to recognize this, but the fact remains that a leaven of humor, sentiment, imagination and tropic nonchalance has gone into the making of the South from a humble, unacknowledged source.

Democracy itself is obstructed and stagnated to the extent that any of its channels are closed.

The pulse of the Negro world has begun to beat in Harlem.

The Younger Generation comes, bringing its gifts. They are the first fruits of the Negro Renaissance. Youth speaks, and the voice of the New Negro is heard.

Audre Lorde

1934–1992 ◆ poet, writer, and literary activist ◆ self-described as a "black feminist lesbian mother poet" ◆ books include *From a Land Where Other People Live*, *The Black Unicorn*, and *Zami: A New Spelling of My Name—A Biomythography*

Art is not living. It is the use of living.

Even the smallest victory is never to be taken for granted. Each victory must be applauded, because it is so easy not to battle at all, to just accept and call that acceptance inevitable.

If I didn't define myself for myself, I would be crunched into other people's fantasies for me and eaten alive.

The white fathers told us, "I think, therefore, I am" and the black mother within each of us—the poet—whispers in our dreams, "I feel, therefore I can be free." Poetry coins the language to express and charter this revolutionary demand.

Divide and conquer, in our world, must become define and empower.

In our work and in our living, we must recognize that difference is a reason for celebration and growth, rather than a reason for destruction.

Every black woman in America lives her life somewhere along a wide curve of ancient and unexpressed anger.

What is there possibly left for us to be afraid of, after we have dealt face to face with death and not embraced it? Once I accept the existence of dying as a life process, who can ever have power over me again?

I write for those women who do not speak, for those who do not have a voice because they were so terrified, because we are taught to respect fear more than ourselves. We've been taught that silence would save us, but it won't.

Only by living in harmony with your contradictions can you keep it all afloat.

We cannot afford to do our enemies' work by destroying each other.

Poetry is not only dream and vision; it is the skeleton architecture of our lives. It lays the foundations for a future of change, a bridge across our fears of what has never been before.

Joe Louis

1914–1981 ◆ "Brown Bomber" ◆ world heavyweight boxing
champion ◆ possibly the first African American to achieve
the status of hero in the U.S. ◆ helped integrate the game of golf
◆ autobiography, *Joe Louis: My Life*

I danced, I paid the piper, and left him a big fat tip.

Every man got a right to his own mistakes. Ain't no man that ain't
made any.

Everything costs a lot of money when you haven't got any.

Everybody wants to go to heaven, but nobody wants to die.

[on being a native of the South] Nobody ever called me nigger until
I got to Detroit.

I don't like money, actually, but it quiets my nerves.

You can run, but you can't hide.

Joseph E. Lowery

Born 1924 ◆ minister and civil rights leader ◆ advocate of
economic justice ◆ close colleague of Martin Luther King, Jr.,
at the SCLC

*[from his benediction at the inauguration of President Barack
Obama]* Lord, in the memory of all the saints, who from their labors
rest, and in the joy of a new beginning, we ask you to help us work
for that day when black will not be asked to get back, when brown
can stick around, when yellow will be mellow, when the red man
can get ahead, and when white will embrace what is right.

If you don't know where you come from, it's difficult to assess where
you are. It's even more difficult to plan where you are going.

Black on black crime is the result of self-hatred. Self-hatred is a
result of our oppression. We can't get back at the folks who oppress
us so we attack ourselves.

America has abandoned the strong woman of spirituality and is
shacking up with the harlot of materialism.

The safest sex is on the shore of abstinence. The next is with one faithful partner. If you insist on wading out into the turbulent waters of multiple sex partners—wear a life jacket.

Martin [Luther King, Jr.] saw the role of a minister as advocate, interpreter and servant. Human rights and the "movement" were not peripheral or tangential aspects of ministry for us, but represented commitment to the kingdom of God which we interpreted as a kingdom of justice, equity and peace.

When the government, by public policy, kept you out, the government has a responsibility, by public policy, to bring you in. And it needs to be just as intentional about including you as it was about excluding you.

Rosa Parks was known as the queen mother of the [civil rights] movement. She sat down so that her people could stand up.

If you can take care of the internal, you can easily take care of the external. Then you can avoid the infernal and latch on to the eternal.

Moms Mabley

c. 1897–1975 ◆ standup comedienne and pioneer of the so-called
"Chitlin' Circuit" of vaudeville ◆ stage and film actress
◆ recordings include *The Funny Sides of Moms Mabley* ◆
plays include *Blackberries of 1932* and *Sidewalks of Harlem* ◆
films include *The Emperor Jones* and *The Cincinnati Kid*

There ain't nothing an old man can do for me except bring me a message from a young one.

Love is like playing checkers. You have to know which man to move.

A woman is a woman until the day she dies, but a man's a man only as long as he can.

If you always do what you always did, you will always get what you always got.

Paule Marshall

Born 1929 ◆ writer, educator, and orator ◆ winner of a MacArthur
Prize Fellowship for lifetime achievement ◆ books include
*Brown Girl, Brownstones, Soul Clap Hands and Sing, Reena, and
Other Short Stories,* and a memoir, *Triangular Road*

[The group of women around the table long ago] . . . taught me my
first lessons in the narrative art. They trained my ear. They set a
standard of excellence. This is why the best of my work must be
attributed to them; it stands as a testimony to the rich legacy of
language and culture they so freely passed on to me in the wordshop
of the kitchen.

Art is inseparable from life, and form and content are one.

Once a great wrong has been done, it never dies. People speak the
words of peace, but their hearts do not forgive. Generations perform
ceremonies of reconciliation but there is no end.

Thurgood Marshall

1908–1993 ◆ jurist and civil rights advocate ◆ chief counsel for the
NAACP who won the victory in *Brown v. Board of Education*
◆ the first African-American supreme court justice

The measure of a country's greatness is its ability to retain compassion in times of crisis. In striking down capital punishment, this
Court does not malign our system of government. On the contrary,
it pays homage to it.

In the short run, it may seem to be the easier course to allow our
great metropolitan areas to be divided up each into two cities—one
white, the other black—but it is a course, I predict, our people will
ultimately regret.

I do not believe that the meaning of the Constitution was forever
"fixed" at the Philadelphia Convention. . . . To the contrary, the
government they devised was defective from the start, requiring
several amendments, a civil war, and momentous social transformation to attain the system of constitutional government, and its
respect for the individual freedoms and human rights we hold as
fundamental today.

I am appalled at the ethical bankruptcy of those who preach a "right to life" that means, under present social policies, a bare existence in utter misery for many poor women and their children.

It must be remembered that during most of the past 200 years, the Constitution as interpreted by this Court did not prohibit the most ingenious and pervasive forms of discrimination against the Negro. Now, when a state acts to remedy the effects of that legacy of discrimination, I cannot believe that this same Constitution stands as a barrier.

[*Brown v. Board of Education*] probably did more than anything else to awaken the Negro from his apathy to demand his right to equality.

A child born to a black mother in a state like Mississippi . . . by merely drawing its first breath in the democracy has exactly the same rights as a white baby born to the wealthiest person in the United States. It's not true, but I challenge anyone to say it is not a goal worth working for.

I have a lifetime appointment and I intend to serve it. I expect to die at 110, shot by a jealous husband.

Provided it is adequately enforced, law can change things for the better; moreover, it can change the hearts of men.

To protest against injustices is the foundation of all our American democracy.

None of us got where we are solely by pulling ourselves up by our bootstraps.

My dad told me way back that you can't use race. For example, there's no difference between a white snake and a black snake. They'll both bite.

If the First Amendment means anything, it means that a State has no business telling a man, sitting alone in his own house, what books he may read or what films he may watch. Our whole constitutional heritage rebels at the thought of giving government the power to control men's minds.

History teaches us that grave threats to liberty often come in times of urgency, when constitutional rights seem too extravagant to endure.

Benjamin E. Mays

1894–1984 ✦ minister, educator, orator, journalist, and reformer
✦ president of Morehouse College, Atlanta ✦ recipient of the
NAACP's Spingarn Medal ✦ autobiography, *Born to Rebel*

He who starts behind in the great race of life must forever remain behind or run faster than the man in front.

It isn't how long one lives, but how well. It's what one accomplishes for mankind that matters. Jesus died at thirty-three; Joan of Arc at nineteen; Byron and Burns at thirty-three; Keats at twenty-five; Marlowe at twenty-nine; Shelley at thirty; Dunbar before thirty-five . . . and Martin Luther King, Jr. at thirty-nine.

The people in the church did not contribute one dime to help me with my education. But they gave me something far more valuable. They gave me encouragement.

The tragedy in life doesn't lie in not reaching your goal. The tragedy lies in having no goal to reach. It isn't a calamity to die with dreams unfulfilled, but it is certainly a calamity not to dream. It is not a disaster to be unable to capture your ideal, but it is a disaster to have no ideal to capture.

I make bold to assert that it took more courage for Martin Luther King, Jr. to practice nonviolence than it took his assassin to fire the fatal shot.

Willie Mays

Born 1931 ✦ major league baseball player ✦ excelled at both
batting and fielding ✦ Baseball Hall of Fame ✦ autobiographies,
Say Hey and *Willie Mays: My Life In and Out of Baseball*

They throw the ball, I hit it. They hit the ball, I catch it.

Baseball is a game, yes. It is also a business. But what it most truly is, is disguised combat. For all its gentility, its almost leisurely pace, baseball is violence under wraps.

Robinson was important to all blacks. To make it into the majors and to take all the name calling, he had to be something special. He had to take all this for years, not just for Jackie Robinson, but for the nation.

Youngsters of Little League can survive under-coaching a lot better than over-coaching.

I was very fortunate to play sports. All the anger in me went out. I had to do what I had to do. If you stay angry all the time, then you really don't have a good life.

Nathan McCall

Born 1955 ◆ writer, educator, lecturer, and civil rights activist
◆ *Washington Post* reporter ◆ books include *Them*, *What's Going On*, and an autobiography, *Makes Me Wanna Holler: A Young Black Man in America*

Some white people are so accustomed to operating at a competitive advantage that when the playing field is level, they feel handicapped.

Although it had been the most tragic event in my life, prison—with all its sickness and suffering—had also been my most instructional challenge. . . . Through that painful trip, I'd found meaning. No longer was life a thing of bewilderment. No longer did I feel like a cosmic freak, a black intruder in a world not created for me and my people.

The mind is like the body. If you don't work actively to protect its health, you can lose it, especially if you're a black man, nineteen years old and wondering, as I was, if you were born into the wrong world.

Hattie McDaniel

1895–1952 ◆ film and radio actress, songwriter, and philanthropist ◆ voice of Beulah on the radio show ◆ first African American to win an Oscar (best supporting actress in *Gone with the Wind*)

My own life even surprises me, although from the time I was six, I have known I wanted to be an actress.

A woman's gifts will make room for her.

Faith is the black person's federal reserve system.

I did my best, and God did the rest.

I've played everything but a harp.

When I was little, my mother taught me how to use a fork and knife. The trouble is that Mother forgot to teach me how to stop using them!

[on being criticized for accepting stereotypical black roles] What do you want me to do? Play a glamour girl and sit on Clark Gable's knee? When you ask me not to play the parts, what have you got in return?

You can best fight any existing evil from the inside.

Claude McKay

1890–1948 ◆ poet, writer, and political activist ◆ author of
Home to Harlem, the first bestselling novel by a Harlem
Renaissance writer ◆ other books include *Spring in
New Hampshire, Harlem Shadows*, and his autobiography,
A Long Way from Home

Nations, like plants and human beings, grow. And if the development is thwarted they are dwarfed and overshadowed.

It's when you're down that you learn about your faults.

All peoples must struggle to live, but just as what was helpful for one man might be injurious to another, so it might be with whole communities of peoples.

Negroes are like trees. They wear all colors naturally.

Human dignity is more precious than prestige.

I know the dark delight of being strange, the penalty of difference in the crowd, the loneliness of wisdom among fools.

Kelly Miller

1863–1939 ◆ writer, mathematician, sociologist, and educator
◆ Dean of Howard University's College of Arts and Sciences
◆ co-edited *The Crisis*, the NAACP journal ◆ books include
Out of the House of Bondage and *Race Adjustment:
The Everlasting Stain*

The Negro pays for what he wants and begs for what he needs.

Circumstances not only alter causes; they alter character.

Crime has no color, the criminal no race. He is the common enemy of society.

When reform becomes impossible, revolution becomes imperative.

Advantage and opportunity confer obligation.

Thelonious Monk

1917–1982 ♦ "Founding Father of Modern Jazz" ♦ jazz pianist,
composer, and arranger ♦ compositions include
"'Round Midnight" and "Straight, No Chaser"

One of the guiding philosophies of music is to find your own voice.

As for the hard times I've had—I've never been jealous of any
musician, or anything. Musicians and other people have told lies on
me, sure, and it has kept me from jobs for a while. . . . But it didn't
bother me. I kept on making it—recording and doing what I'm
doing, and thinking. While they were talking, I was thinking music
and still trying to play.

I was about nineteen to twenty, I guess, when I started to hear my
music in my mind. So I had to compose music in order to express
the type of ideas that I had. Because the music wasn't on the scene.
It had to be composed. . . . I just composed music that fit with how
I was thinking. . . . I didn't want to play the way I'd heard music
played all my life. I got tired of hearing that. I wanted to hear something else, something better.

Bebop wasn't developed in any deliberate way.

I hit the piano with my elbow sometimes because of a certain sound
I want to hear, certain chords. You can't hit that many notes with
your hands.

There are no wrong notes.

Anne Moody

Born 1940 ♦ writer and civil rights activist ♦ worked with CORE,
NAACP, and SNCC during the civil rights movement of the sixties
♦ autobiography, *Coming of Age in Mississippi*

Before Emmett Till's murder, I had known the fear of hunger, hell,
and the Devil. But now there was a new fear known to me—the fear
of being killed just because I was black. This was the worst of my
fears.

The universal fight for human rights, dignity, justice, equality, and freedom is not and should not be just the fight of the American Negro or the Indians or the Chicanos. It's the fight of every ethnic and racial minority, every suppressed and exploited person, every one of the millions who daily suffer one or another of the indignities of the powerless and voiceless masses.

Toni Morrison

Born 1931 ◆ writer, educator, and editor ◆ books include
The Bluest Eye, Song of Solomon (winner of the National Book
Critics Circle Award), and *Beloved* (winner of the Pulitzer Prize for
Fiction) ◆ the first African-American woman to win the
Nobel Prize in Literature

A man ain't nothing but a man, but a son? Well now, that's *somebody*.

If you can't count, they can cheat you. If you can't read, they can beat you.

Along with the idea of romantic love, she was introduced to another — physical beauty. Probably the most destructive ideas in the history of human thought. Both originated in envy, thrived in insecurity, and ended in disillusion.

The reclamation of racial beauty in the sixties . . . was not a reaction to the self-mocking, humorous critique of cultural/racial foibles common in all groups, but against the damaging internalization of assumptions of immutable inferiority originating in an outside gaze.

The best art is political and you ought to be able to make it unquestionably political and irrevocably beautiful at the same time.

When a man angers you, he conquers you.

You are confined by your own system of oppression.

It's not because one is black that the prejudice exists. The prejudice exists because one can identify the person who was once a slave or in a lower class, and the caste system can survive longer. In Nazi Germany, they found a way to identify the Jews by putting a label on them to indicate who they were . . . But here you have people who are black.

Race has become metaphorical, a way of referring to and disguising forces, events, classes, and expressions of social decay and economic division far more threatening to the body politic than biological "race" ever was.

She gather me, man. The pieces I am, she gather them and give them back to me in all the right order. It's good, you know, when you got a woman who is a friend of your mind.

We are very practical people, very down-to-earth, even shrewd people. But with that practicality we also accepted what I suppose could be called superstition and magic, which is another way of knowing things.

Black people's grace has been what they do with language.

We die. That may be the meaning of life. But we do have language. That may be the measure of our lives.

Liberation means you don't have to be silenced.

The ability of writers to imagine what is not the self, to familiarize the strange and mystify the familiar, is the test of their power.

"Jelly Roll" Morton

c. 1890–1941 ◆ self-described "Originator of Jazz" ◆ musician, composer, and bandleader ◆ genres included ragtime, Dixieland, and swing ◆ played with the Red Hot Peppers and the New Orleans Rhythm Kings ◆ his classic songs include "Black Bottom Stomp" and "Wild Man Blues"

I invented jazz in 1902.

Get up from that piano. You hurtin' its feelings.

Not until 1926 did they get a fair idea of real jazz, when I decided to live in New York.

[*on his system of jazz notation*] I myself figured out the peculiar form of mathematics and harmonies that was strange to all the world but me.

Jazz started in New Orleans.

My contributions were many: First clown director, with witty sayings and flashily dressed, now called master of ceremonies; first glee club in orchestra; the first washboard was recorded by me; bass fiddle, drums—which was supposed to be impossible to record.

I have been robbed of three million dollars all told. Everyone today is playing my stuff and I don't even get credit. Kansas City style, Chicago style, New Orleans style—hell, they're all Jelly Roll style.

Some blues is played; some is wrote; and some is just tooken.

[My grandmother] told me that devil music would surely bring about my downfall, but I just couldn't put it behind me.

Elijah Muhammad

1897–1975 ♦ a.k.a. Elijah Poole ♦ religious leader, writer, and entrepreneur ♦ Founder of the Nation of Islam, the black separatist religious group ♦ books include *Message to the Blackman in America*

We cannot be equal with the master until we own what the master owns. We cannot be equal with the master until we have the freedom the master enjoys. We cannot be equal with the master until we have the education the master has. Then, we can say, "Master, recognize us as your equal."

It is hard to apply oneself to study. We have been to their schools and gone as far as they allowed us to go.

Knowledge of one's identity, one's self, community, nation, religion, and God, is the true meaning of resurrection, while ignorance of it signifies hell.

Not one of us will have to raise a sword. Not one gun would we need to fire. The great cannon that will be fired is our unity.

Discard your former slave-master's names and be willing and ready to accept one of Allah's Pure and Righteous Names that He Alone will give our people from His Own Mouth! A good name is, indeed, better than gold.

Gloria Naylor

Born 1950 ♦ writer, educator, and lecturer ♦ novels include *The Women of Brewster Place* (winner of the American Book Award), *Mama Day*, and *Bailey's Cafe*

Sometimes being a friend means mastering the art of timing. There is a time for silence. A time to let go and allow people to hurl themselves into their own destiny. And a time to prepare to pick up the pieces when it's all over.

I am alive because of the blood of proud people who never scraped or begged or apologized for what they were. They lived asking only one thing of this world—to be allowed to be. And I learned through the blood of these people that black isn't beautiful and it isn't ugly— black is!

I got nothing, but you welcome to all of that.

Linden Hills wasn't black; it was successful. The shining surface of their careers . . . only reflected the bright nothing that was inside of them.

I don't believe that life is supposed to make you feel good, or to make you feel miserable either. Life is just supposed to make you feel.

Larry Neal

1937–1981 ◆ poet, playwright, arts critic, educator, and scholar
◆ notable of the Black Arts Movement ◆ co-editor with Amiri
Baraka of the anthology *Black Fire: An Anthology of
Afro-American Writing*

America is the world's greatest jailer, and we all in jails. Black spirits contained like magnificent birds of wonder.

The Black Arts Movement [is] the aesthetic and spiritual sister of the Black Power concept. As such it envisions an art that speaks directly to the needs and aspirations of Black America.

The artist and the political activist are one. They are both shapers of the future reality. Both understand and manipulate the collective myths of the race. Both are warriors, priests, lovers, and destroyers.

Boxing is just another kind of rhythm activity. Like all sports is based on rhythm. Dig: if you ain't got no rhythm, you can't play no sports.

The black Holy Ghost roaring into some shack of a church, in the South, seizing the congregation with an ancient energy and power—the black church, therefore, represents and embodies the transplanted African memory.

William C. Nell

1816–1874 ♦ abolitionist, journalist, orator, and historian ♦ author
of a pamphlet, *Services of Colored Americans in the Wars of 1776
and 1812*, one of the first works of African-American history, and a
book, *The Colored Patriots of the American Revolution*

Our brethren at the South should not be called slaves, but prisoners
of war.

I have borne allegiance to principles, rather than men.

The treatment of the colored man in this country is a legitimate
illustration of "hating those whom we have injured."

Aroused by the American Antislavery Society, the very white man
who had forgotten and denied the claim of the black man to the
rights of humanity, now thunder that claim at every gate, from
cottage to capitol, from schoolhouse to university, from the railroad
carriage to the house of God.

The various conflicts by sea and land, which have challenged the
energies of the United States, have been signalized by the devotion
and bravery of colored Americans, despite the persecutions heaped,
Olympus high, upon them, by their fellow countrymen. They have
ever proved loyal, and ready to worship or die, if need be, at
Freedom's shrine.

Huey P. Newton

1942–1989 ♦ radical activist, co-founder of the Black Panther Party
and its minister of defense ♦ books include *To Die for the People*
and *Revolutionary Suicide*

I do not expect the white media to create positive black male
images.

Black people already know they're poor and powerless. They just
don't understand the nature of their oppression. They haven't drawn
the line from their condition to the *system* of capitalism.

I suggested that we use the panther as our symbol and call our
political vehicle the Black Panther Party. The panther is a fierce
animal, but he will not attack unless he is backed into a corner; then
he will strike out.

The first lesson a revolutionary must learn is that he is a doomed man.

The police have never been our protectors. . . . With weapons in our hands, we were no longer their subjects but their equals.

I know sociologically that words, the power of the word, words stigmatize people. We felt that the police needed a label, a label other than that fear image that they carried in the community. So we used the pig as the rather low-lifed animal in order to identify the police. And it worked.

I think what motivates people is not great hate, but great love for other people.

You can jail a Revolutionary, but you can't jail the Revolution.

My fear was not of death itself, but a death without meaning.

Eleanor Holmes Norton

Born 1937 ◆ lawyer, civil rights activist, politician, feminist, educator, and radio and TV personality ◆ worked for SNCC and the Mississippi Freedom Democratic Party during the civil rights movement of the sixties ◆ attorney for the ACLU ◆ District of Columbia's elected delegate to the U.S. Congress

Men without jobs do not form families.

Affirmative action, by all statistical measures, has been the central ingredient to the creation of the black middle class.

There are not many males, black or white, who wish to get involved with a woman who's committed to her own development.

On the road to equality there is no better place for blacks to detour around American values than in forgoing its example in the treatment of its women and the organization of its family.

With children no longer the universally accepted reason for marriage, marriages are going to have to exist on their own merits.

The only way to make sure people you agree with can speak is to support the rights of people you don't agree with.

The country would go bankrupt in a day if the Supreme Court suddenly ordered the powers-that-be to pay back wages to children of slaves and to the women who've worked all their lives for half wages or no pay.

One ought to struggle for its own sake. One ought to be against racism and sexism because they are wrong, not because one is black or one is female.

Shaquille O'Neal

Born 1972 ◆ athlete, rapper, actor, and philanthropist ◆ one of NBA's top fifty players of all time ◆ albums include *Shaq Diesel*, *You Can't Stop the Reign*, and *Respect* ◆ films include *Kazaam*, *He Got Game*, and *The Brothers*

People try to limit me, but I would never limit myself. I could never do just one thing, especially if I have the opportunity to do more.

I'm tired of hearing about money, money, money, money, money. I just want to play the game, drink Pepsi, wear Reebok.

I don't believe that I personally have been changed by the money. . . . The bad thing is people *assume* you've changed because now you have money.

I did everything the right way and earned my spot in this game; nothing was given to me.

I realize that I am a role model. . . . The best thing for me and other athletes is to stay out of trouble.

Barack Hussein Obama

Born 1961 ◆ writer, attorney, orator, and politician ◆ 44th president of the United States, the first African American to hold the office ◆ books include *The Audacity of Hope*, and a memoir, *Dreams from My Father*

My job is not to represent Washington to you, but to represent you to Washington.

There's not a liberal America and a conservative America; there's the United States of America.

What Washington needs is adult supervision.

Focusing your life solely on making a buck shows a certain poverty of ambition.

To those leaders around the globe who seek to sow conflict, or blame their society's ills on the West—know that your people will judge you on what you can build, not what you destroy. To those who cling to power through corruption and deceit and the silencing of dissent, know that you are on the wrong side of history; but that we will extend a hand if you are willing to unclench your fist.

It is easier to start wars than to end them. It is easier to blame others than to look inward; to see what is different about someone than to find the things we share. . . . There is also one rule that lies at the heart of every religion—that we do unto others as we would have them do unto us.

[*Veterans Day*] We mark this day as a celebration of those who made victory possible. . . . Because they did, our country still stands; our founding principles still shine; nations around the world that once knew nothing but fear now know the blessings of freedom. That is why we fight—in hopes of a day when we no longer need to. And that is why we gather at these solemn remembrances and reminders of war—to recommit ourselves to the hard work of peace.

I've got two daughters. Nine years old and six years old. I am going to teach them first of all about values and morals. But if they make a mistake, I don't want them punished with a baby.

No one is pro-abortion.

My faith is one that admits some doubt.

Americans . . . still believe in an America where anything's possible—they just don't think their leaders do.

Change will not come if we wait for some other person or some other time. We are the ones we've been waiting for. We are the change that we seek.

If the people cannot trust their government to do the job for which it exists—to protect them and to promote their common welfare—all else is lost.

Poorly secured nuclear material in the former Soviet Union, or secrets from a scientist in Pakistan, could help build a bomb that detonates in Paris. The poppies in Afghanistan become the heroin in Berlin. The poverty and violence in Somalia breeds the terror of tomorrow.

Today we are engaged in a deadly global struggle with those who would intimidate, torture, and murder people for exercising the most basic freedoms. If we are to win this struggle and spread those freedoms, we must keep our own moral compass pointed in a true direction.

And so, to all other peoples and governments . . . from the grandest capitals to the small village where my father was born: know that America is a friend of each nation and every man, woman and child who seeks a future of peace and dignity, and we are ready to lead once more.

After a century of striving, after a year of debate, after an historic vote, health care reform is no longer an unmet promise. It is the law of the land.

Get involved in an issue that you're passionate about. It almost doesn't matter what it is—improving the school system, developing strategies to wean ourselves off foreign oil, expanding health care for kids. We give too much of our power away, to the professional politicians, to the lobbyists, to cynicism. And our democracy suffers as a result.

[on improving education in America] Nothing has a bigger impact than reading to children early in life. Obviously we all have a personal obligation to turn off the TV and read to our own children; but beyond that, participating in a literacy program, working with parents who themselves have difficulty reading, helping their children with their literacy skills, can make a huge difference in a child's life.

This is the moment when we must come together to save the planet. Let us resolve that we will not leave our children a world where the oceans rise and famine spreads and terrible storms devastate our lands.

My parents shared not only an improbable love, they shared an abiding faith in the possibilities of this nation. They would give me an African name, Barack, or blessed, believing that in a tolerant America your name is no barrier to success.

[on America] It's the hope of slaves sitting around a fire singing freedom songs; the hope of immigrants setting out for distant shores . . . the hope of a skinny kid with a funny name who believes that America has a place for him, too. The audacity of hope!

Michelle Robinson Obama

Born 1964 ◆ lawyer, administrator (in the Chicago city
government), and community activist ◆ associate dean of
student services at the University of Chicago, and later,
vice president for community and external affairs at the
University of Chicago hospitals ◆
the first African-American First Lady

All of us driven by a simple belief that the world as it is just won't do . . . have an obligation to fight for the world as it should be.

The truth is, in order to get things like universal health care and a revamped education system . . . someone is going to have to give up a piece of their pie so that someone else can have more.

One of the lessons I grew up with was to always stay true to yourself and never let what somebody else says distract you from your goals. And so when I hear about negative and false attacks, I really don't invest any energy in them, because I know who I am.

My first job . . . is going to continue to be mom-in-chief. Making sure that . . . [our girls] know they will continue to be the center of our universe.

For the first time in my adult life, I am proud of my country because it feels like hope is finally making a comeback.

I want to leave something behind so that we can say, "Because of this time that this person spent here, this thing has changed." And my hope is that that's going to be in the area of childhood obesity.

[Barack and I believe] that you work hard for what you want in life, that your word is your bond, and you do what you say you're going to do, that you treat people with dignity and respect, even if you don't know them, and even if you don't agree with them.

Jesse Owens

1913–1980 ◆ track and field athlete, disk jockey, entrepreneur, and
inspirational speaker ◆ won four gold medals at the 1936 Berlin
Olympics, a stunning rebuke to Hitler's notions of Aryan superiority
◆ recipient of both the Presidential Medal of Freedom and the
Living Legend awards ◆ autobiography, *Jesse: The Man Who
Outran Hitler*

Find the good. It's all around you. Find it, showcase it, and you'll
start believing in it.

For a time, at least, I was the most famous person in the entire
world.

Friendships are born on the field of athletic strife and are the real
gold of competition. Awards become corroded, friends gather no
dust.

You see, *black* isn't beautiful. *White* isn't beautiful. Skin-deep is
never beautiful.

In theory, the Emancipation Proclamation had been a wonderful
thing. But in 1915 in Alabama, it was only a theory. The Negro
had been set free to work eighteen hours a day, free to see all his
labor add up to a debt at the year's end, free to be chained to the
land he tilled, but could never own any more than if he were still
a slave.

[After the Olympics] I came back to my native country and I
couldn't ride in the front of the bus. I had to go to the back door. I
couldn't live where I wanted.

[My gold medals] have kept me alive over the years. Time has stood
still for me. That golden moment dies hard.

Any black who strives to achieve in this country should think in
terms of not only himself but also how he can reach down and grab
another black child and pull him to the top of the mountain where
he is.

One chance is all you need.

Leroy "Satchel" Paige

c. 1906–1982 ◆ first of the Negro League players to be inducted into the Baseball Hall of Fame ◆ in his forties, he was the seventh African American to be recruited into the major leagues after Jackie Robinson broke the color barrier ◆ autobiography, *Maybe I'll Pitch Forever*

How old would you be if you didn't know how old you was?

Age is a question of mind over matter. If you don't mind, it don't matter.

I never rush myself. See, they can't start the game without me.

I never threw an illegal pitch. The trouble is, once in a while I toss one that ain't never been seen by this generation.

Just take the ball and throw it where you want to. Throw strikes. Home plate don't move.

My pitching philosophy is simple—keep the ball 'way from the bat.

[On pitching] It's such a thing as I practiced all the time; I just *practiced* control. Anything you practice you begin to come good at, regardless of what it is.

When a batter swings and I see his knees move, I can tell just what his weaknesses are; then I just put the ball where I know he can't hit it.

[Satchel's Rules for Staying Young] 1. Avoid fried meats, which angry up the blood. 2. If your stomach disputes you, lie down and pacify it with cool thoughts. 3. Keep the juices flowing by jangling around gently as you move. 4. Go very light on the vices such as carrying on in society. The social rumble ain't restful. 5. Avoid running at all times. 6. Don't look back. Something might be gaining on you.

Not to be cheered by praise, not to be grieved by blame, but to know thoroughly one's own virtues or powers are the characteristics of an excellent man.

Work like you don't need the money. Love like you've never been hurt. Dance like nobody's watching.

With women, it's like this: I'm not married, but I'm in great demand.

It got so I could nip frosting off a cake with my fastball.

Never let your head hang down. Never give up and sit down and grieve. Find another way. And don't pray when it rains if you don't pray when the sun shines.

Ain't no man can avoid being born average, but there ain't no reason a man got to be common.

Charlie Parker

1920–1955 ◆ "Bird" ◆ alto saxophone player, composer, and modern jazz icon ◆ compositions include "A Night in Tunisia," "Ornithology," and "Yardbird Suite"

Music is your own experience, your own thoughts, your wisdom. If you don't live it, it won't come out of your horn. They teach you there's a boundary line to music. But, man, there's no boundary line to art.

Don't play the saxophone. Let it play you.

I realized by using the high notes of the chords as a melodic line, and by the right harmonic progression, I could play what I heard inside me. That's when I was born.

You've got to learn your instrument. Then, you practice, practice, practice. And then, when you finally get up there on the bandstand, forget all that and just wail.

I put quite a bit of study into the horn . . . In fact, the neighbors threatened to ask my mother to move once . . . She said I was driving them crazy with the horn. I used to put in at least eleven to fifteen hours a day.

I am a devout musician.

Let's celebrate. We have Bartók and gin—what else do we need?

Any musician who says he is playing better either on tea [marijuana], the needle, or when he is juiced, is a plain straight liar. . . . You can miss the most important years of your life, the years of possible creation.

Gordon Parks

1912–2006 ◆ photographer, poet, writer, filmmaker, and composer
◆ staff photographer for *Life* ◆ films include *Shaft, Shaft's Big
Score,* and *Leadbelly* ◆ books include *The Learning Tree,*
A *Poet and His Camera,* and A *Hungry Heart*

All our lives we have cloaked our feelings, bided our time, waited for
the year, the month, the day and the hour when we could do
without fear, at last, what we are doing just now.

The guy who takes a chance, who walks the line between the known
and the unknown, who is unafraid of failure, will succeed.

America is me. It gave me the only life I know, so I must share in its
survival.

Steep yourself in black history, but don't stop there. I love Duke
Ellington and Count Basie, but I also listen to Bach and Beethoven.
Do not allow yourself to be trapped and snared in limits set for you
by someone else.

Until my mid-teens I lived in fear: fear of being shot, lynched or
beaten to death—and not for any wrongdoing of my own. I could
easily have been the victim of mistaken identity or of an act of terror
by hate-filled men.

[Growing up in Kansas] I was called "nigger," "black boy," "darkey,"
"shine" and all those other names that arouse anger and humiliation. I was stoned and beaten. The indignities came so often that I
soon began to accept them as normal. But I always fought back. In
retrospect, I consider myself lucky to be alive . . . I also consider
myself lucky that I didn't kill someone.

I have learned that the subtle art of rejection, used with finesse, can
be every bit as abusive as a punch in the face.

There is nothing ignoble about a black man climbing from the
troubled darkness on a white man's ladder, providing he doesn't
forsake the others who, subsequently, must escape the same
darkness.

I had to constantly overcome the disadvantages of having no
academic training by inventing my own way of doing things.

Success can be wracking and reproachful, to you and those close to
you. It can entangle you with legends that are consuming and all but
impossible to live up to.

If a man can reach the latter days of his life with his soul intact, he has mastered life.

Rosa Parks

1913–2005 ◆ "Mother of the Modern Day Civil Rights Movement"
◆ seamstress, writer, and civil rights activist ◆ founder of the Rosa
and Raymond Parks Institute for Self Development ◆ recipient of
the Medal of Freedom Award ◆ books include *Rosa Parks:
My Story* and *The Autobiography of Rosa Parks*

We didn't have any of what they called Civil Rights back then. It was just a matter of survival—existing from day to day.

[on her refusal to give up her bus seat] When I made that decision, I knew I had the strength of my ancestors with me.

When people made up their minds that they wanted to be free and took action, then there was a change.

My mother believed in freedom and equality even though we didn't know it for reality during our life in Alabama.

I was determined to achieve the total freedom that our history lessons taught us we were entitled to, no matter what the sacrifice.

Each person must live their life as a model for others.

People always say that I didn't give up my seat because I was tired, but that isn't true. I was not tired physically, or no more tired than I usually was at the end of a working day. I was not old, although some people have an image of me as being old then. I was forty-two. No, the only tired I was, was tired of giving in.

Floyd Patterson

1935–2006 ◆ world heavyweight championship boxer ◆ winner of
an Olympic gold medal ◆ Boxing Hall of Fame ◆ memoir,
Victory Over Myself

It's easy to do anything in victory. It's in defeat that a man reveals himself.

They said I was the fighter who got knocked down the most, but I also got up the most.

When you have millions of dollars, you have millions of friends.

Fear was absolutely necessary. Without it, I would have been scared to death.

There is so much hate among people, so much contempt inside people who'd like you to think they're moral, but they have to hire prizefighters to do their hating for them. And we do. We get into a ring and act out other people's hates.

The fighter loses more than his pride in the fight; he loses part of his future. He's a step closer to the slum he came from.

[Boxing] is like being in love with a woman . . . it can do me all kinds of harm but I love it.

Ann Petry

1908–1997 ◆ poet, writer, children's book author, educator, and feminist ◆ books include *The Street*, the first novel by an African-American woman to become a bestseller, *Miss Muriel and Other Stories*, and *Harriet Tubman: Conductor on the Underground Railroad*

The men stood around and the women worked. The men left the women and the women went on working and the kids were left alone. Alone. Always alone. They wouldn't stay in the house after school because they were afraid in the empty, silent, dark rooms. . . . And the street reached out and sucked them up.

The instant they saw the color of her skin they knew what she must be like; they were so confident about what she must be like they didn't need to know her personally in order to verify their estimate.

Streets like 116th Street [in Harlem] or being colored, or a combination of both with all that implied, had turned Pop into a sly old man who drank too much; had killed Mom off when she was in her prime.

She was going to stake out a piece of life for herself. She had come this far poor and black and shut out as though a door had been slammed in her face. Well, she would shove it open; she would beat and bang on it and push against it and use a chisel in order to get it open.

I was a black woman at a point in time when being a writer was not usual, and I was besieged. Everyone wanted a part of me.

William Pickens

1881–1954 ◆ writer, orator, journalist, and civil rights activist
◆ associate field secretary for the NAACP ◆ contributing editor
of the Associated Negro Press ◆ autobiography, *Bursting
Bounds: The Autobiography of a "New Negro"*

The very advantages of a democracy make disenfranchisement therein the worst of tyrannies.

Those who quote providence are almost without exception the Negro's most active enemies.

The runaway Negro was the vanguard, the first hero in the struggle to free his race.

An insignificant right becomes important when it is assailed.

[My grandmother] lived for forty years with a broken back, the upper part of her body being carried in a horizontal position, at right angles to her lower limbs . . . This was one of the results of slavery. Being a high-tempered house-servant in that system she had been beaten and struck across the back with a stick.

Color had been made the mark of enslavement and was taken to be also the mark of inferiority; for prejudice does not reason, or it would not be prejudice. . . . If prejudice could reason, it would dispel itself.

The best time to do a thing is when it can be done.

Sidney Poitier

Born 1927 ◆ actor of stage, screen, and TV, film director,
Bahamian ambassador to Japan, and civil rights activist
◆ first African American to win an Academy Award for
Best Actor ◆ awarded the Presidential Medal of
Freedom ◆ autobiography, *The Measure of a Man:
A Spiritual Autobiography*

The measure of a man is how well he provides for his children.

Most of my career unfolded in the 1960s, which was one of the periods in American history with certain attitudes toward minorities that stayed in vogue. I didn't understand the elements swirling around. I was a young actor with some talent, an enormous curiosity, and a certain kind of appeal. You wrap all that together and you have a potent mix.

As a man, I've been representative of the values I hold dear. And the values I hold dear are carryovers from the lives of my parents.

Mine was an easy ride compared to Jackie Robinson's.

There is not racial or ethnic domination of hopelessness. It's everywhere.

If you apply reason and logic to this career of mine, you're not going to get very far.

They call me *Mister* Tibbs.

Adam Clayton Powell, Jr.

1908–1972 ✦ pastor, politician, writer, lecturer, and civil rights leader ✦ first African American elected to the New York City Council ✦ U.S. congressman ✦ co-founder of the newspaper, *People's Voice* ✦ books include *Keep the Faith, Baby!* and his autobiography, *Adam by Adam*

I am the product of the sustained indignation of a branded grandfather, the militant protest of my grandmother, the disciplined resentment of my father and mother, and the power of the mass action of the church.

There was only one thing I could do—hammer relentlessly, continually, crying aloud, even if in a wilderness, and force open, by sheer muscle power, every closed door.

No one can say that Christianity has failed. It has never been tried.

Let's trace the birth of an idea. It's born as rampant radicalism, then it becomes progressivism, then liberalism, then it becomes moderate, conservative, outmoded, and gone.

There is no future for a people who deny their past.

We have produced a world of contented bodies and discontented minds.

A man's respect for law and order exists in precise relationship to the size of his paycheck.

Mix a conviction with a man and something happens.

There is no heaven or hell in the sense that they are places one goes after death. The heaven or hell to which one goes is right there in the span of years we spend in this body on earth.

Keep the faith, baby!

Colin Powell

Born 1937 ◆ career soldier who became a four-star general, statesman, and lecturer ◆ government positions included national security advisor, first African American to be chairman of the Joint Chiefs of Staff, and secretary of state ◆ autobiography, *My American Journey*

[*on the consequences of invading Iraq*] Once you break it, you are going to own it, and we're going to be responsible for 26 million people standing there looking at us. And it's going to suck up a good forty to fifty percent of the Army for years. And it's going to take the oxygen out of the political environment.

Many interviewers when they come to talk to me, think they're being progressive by not mentioning in their stories any longer that I'm black. I tell them, "Don't stop now. If I shot somebody you'd mention it."

Let [racism] be a problem to someone else. . . . Let it drag them down. Don't use it as an excuse for your own shortcomings.

The U.S. Constitution is a remarkable document—and a demanding one for those of us who choose to make our career in the military. We are required to pledge our sacred honor to a document that looks at the military as a necessary but undesirable institution useful in times of crisis and to be watched carefully at all other times.

Role models can be black. Rode models can be white. Role models can be generals. Role models can be principals, teachers, doctors, or just your parent who brought you into this world and who is trying to give you the best of everything.

All work is honorable. Always do your best because someone is watching.

There are no more major civil rights laws to be passed. What we are dealing with now is changing of hearts, changing of perspective and of minds.

> *[What follows is a selection from "Colin Powell's Rules" on his desk at the Pentagon.]*

- It ain't as bad as you think. It will look better in the morning.

- Avoid having your ego so close to your position that, when your position fails, your ego goes with it.

- Don't let adverse facts stand in the way of a good decision.

- You can't make someone else's choices. You shouldn't let someone else make yours.

- Don't take counsel of your fears or naysayers.

- Perpetual optimism is a force multiplier.

Leontyne Price

Born 1927 ◆ "Girl with the Golden Voice" ◆ Metropolitan Opera singer (soprano) ◆ first African American to achieve an international reputation in opera ◆ winner of thirteen Grammy Awards and the Presidential Medal of Freedom ◆ operas include *Porgy and Bess, Tosca,* and *Aida,* her signature role

All token blacks have the same experience. I have been pointed at as a solution to things that have not yet begun to be solved, because pointing at us token blacks eases the conscience of millions.

If you are going to think black, think positive about it. Don't think down on it, or think it is something in your way. And this way, when you really do want to stretch out, and express how beautiful black is, everybody will hear you.

The voice is so special. You have to guard it with care, to let nothing disturb it, so you don't lose the bloom, don't let it fade, don't let the petals drop.

If you're not feeling good about you, what you're wearing outside doesn't mean a thing.

The ultimate of being successful is the luxury of giving yourself the time to do what you want to do.

Charley Pride

Born 1938 ✦ singer, guitarist, entrepreneur, and baseball player
✦ first African-American country music singer ✦ for his label RCA,
second only to Elvis Presley in sales ✦ inducted into the Country
Music Hall of Fame and the Grand Ole Opry ✦ autobiography,
Pride: The Charley Pride Story

No one had ever told me that whites were supposed to sing one kind
of music and blacks another—I sang what I liked in the only voice I
had.

The time I spent thinking about how I was better than somebody
else or worrying about somebody else's attitude was time I could put
to better use.

For most entertainers, there is a single experience, one defining
moment, when confidence replaces the self-doubt that most of us
wrestle with.

Richard Pryor

1940–2005 ✦ comedian, actor, writer, and TV personality
✦ screenwriting credits include *Blazing Saddles* and *Car Wash*
✦ Grammy award-winner for his comedy albums and first recipient
of the Mark Twain Prize for American Humor ✦ autobiography,
Pryor Convictions and Other Life Sentences

It's so much easier for me to talk about my life in front of two
thousand people than it is one-to-one. I'm a real defensive person
because if you were sensitive in my neighborhood you were something to eat.

Uninterested in relationships, I caught women as if they were taxis.

I'll never forget going up to Harlem and seeing all those black
people. Jesus, just knowing there were that many of us made me feel
better.

Art is the ability to tell the truth, especially about oneself.

When you ain't got no money, you gotta get an attitude.

Life doesn't change when you start making money; you have the
same problems you always had.

I had some great things and I had some bad things. The best and the worst. In other words, I had a life.

I'm getting paid to make an ass out of myself. What's your excuse?

Robert Purvis

1810–1898 ◆ radical abolitionist, orator, and writer ◆ co-founder of the American Antislavery Society and active in the Underground Railroad (aided about 9,000 fugitive slaves) ◆ works include the pamphlet, *Appeal of Forty Thousand Citizens, Threatened with Disfranchisement*

This is the red man's country by natural right, and the black man's by virtue of his suffering toil.

It is the safeguard of the strongest that he lives under a government which is obliged to respect the voice of the weakest. When you have taken from an individual his right to vote, you have made the government, in regard to him, a mere despotism; and you have taken a step towards making it a despotism to all.

To make me believe that those men who have regulated education in our country have humanity in their hearts is to make me believe a lie.

We are not intruders here nor were our ancestors. Surely you ought to bear as unrepiningly the evil consequences of your fathers' guilt, as we those of our fathers' misfortune.

Asa Philip Randolph

1889–1979 ◆ civil rights and labor leader ◆ organized the 1941 march on Washington to protest discrimination for defense industry jobs and segregation in the military, and the 1963 march on Washington for jobs and freedom ◆ founder of the Brotherhood of Sleeping Car Porters, the first African-American union in the U.S.

A community is democratic only when the humblest and weakest person can enjoy the highest civil, economic, and social rights that the biggest and most powerful possess.

Violence seldom accomplishes permanent and desired results. Herein lies the futility of war.

If the great laboring masses of people, black and white, are kept forever snarling over the question as to who is superior or inferior, they will take a long time to combine for achievement of a common benefit.

In politics, as in other things, there is no such thing as one getting something for nothing. The payoff may involve compromises of various types that may strike at the ideals and principles one has held dear all his life.

The regnant law of the life of political parties, like all other organisms, is self-preservation. They behave in obedience to the principle of the *greatest gain for the least effort.*

White and black workers . . . must be organized together, as the fingers on my hand when they are doubled up in the form of a fist.

Salvation for a race, nation, or class must come from within. Freedom is never granted; it is won. Justice is never given; it is exacted.

J. Saunders Redding

1906–1988 ◆ literary critic, historian, and educator ◆ first African American to hold a faculty position at an Ivy League university (Brown) ◆ his first book, *To Make a Poet Black*, was a groundbreaking work in African-American literary criticism ◆ memoir, *No Day of Triumph*

Sails unfurled, flag drooping at her rounded stern, she rode the tide in from the sea. She was a strange ship, indeed, by all accounts, a frightening ship, a ship of mystery. . . . The flag she flew was Dutch; her crew a motley. Her port of call, an English settlement, Jamestown, in the colony of Virginia [in 1619]. She came, she traded, and shortly afterwards was gone. Probably no ship in modern history has carried a more portentous freight. Her cargo? Twenty slaves.

Literary expression for the Negro has not been, and is not wholly now an art in the sense that the poetry and prose of another people, say the Irish, is art. Almost from the very beginning the literature of the Negro has been literature either of purpose or necessity . . . [as] he became the sometimes frenzied propagandist of racial consciousness and advancement

Ishmael Reed

Born 1938 ◆ poet, writer, dramatist, blues songwriter, and educator
◆ one of the founders of the *East Village Other* ◆ co-founder of the
Before Columbus Foundation which promotes and disseminates
American multicultural literature ◆ books include *Mumbo Jumbo*
and *Reckless Eyeballing*

I try to do what has never been done before.

No one says a novel has to be one thing. It can be anything it wants
to be, a vaudeville show, the six o'clock news, the mumblings of wild
men saddled by demons.

Being a black man in America is like being a spectator at your own
lynching.

All art must be for the end of liberating the masses. A landscape is
only good when it shows the oppressor hanging from a tree.

The Afro-American artist is . . . a conjurer who works JuJu upon
his oppressors; a witch doctor who frees his fellow victims from
the psychic attack launched by demons of the outer and inner
world.

We learn about one another's culture the same way we learn about
sex: in the streets.

I'm not so much influenced by literary influences but by jazz, and
talk radio formats, and television, and, I eavesdrop. . . . I'm orga-
nizing people's thoughts, like overheard conversations in airports
and things like that, and putting them together.

The devil was created by fourth century Christian writers. You don't
find the devil in any African system that I know of, because the
African systems are pantheistic.

Writing has made me a better man. It has put me in contact with
those fleeting moments which prove the existence of soul.

Condoleezza Rice

Born 1954 ✦ government official, professor, diplomat, writer, and
pianist ✦ national security advisor and first African-American
woman to serve as U.S. secretary of state ✦ books include
Condoleezza Rice: A Memoir of My Extraordinary,
Ordinary Family and Me

People may oppose you, but when they realize you can hurt them,
they'll join your side.

I remember the bombing of that Sunday School . . . in Birmingham
in 1963. I did not see it happen, but I heard it happen, and I felt it
happen, just a few blocks away at my father's church. It is a sound
that I will never forget, that will forever reverberate in my ears. That
bomb took the lives of four young girls, including my friend and
playmate, Denise McNair. The crime was calculated to suck the
hope out of young lives, bury their aspirations. But those fears were
not propelled forward, those terrorists failed.

It's bad policy to speculate on what you'll do if a plan fails when
you're trying to make a plan work.

The problem here is that there will always be some uncertainty
about how quickly Saddam can acquire nuclear weapons. But we
don't want the smoking gun to be a mushroom cloud.

We need a common enemy to unite us.

Paul Robeson

1898–1976 ✦ singer, actor of stage and screen, scholar, athlete,
political radical, and civil rights activist ✦ plays include *Othello,*
The Emperor Jones, and *All God's Chillun Got Wings* ✦ films
include *Show Boat* (where he sang "Ol' Man River"), *Song of*
Freedom, and *Tales of Manhattan* ✦ memoir, *Here I Stand*

I heard my people singing!—in the glow of the parlor coal-stove and
on summer porches sweet with lilac air, from choir loft and Sunday
morning pews—and my soul was filled with their harmonies.

Africa is a Dark Continent not merely because its people are dark-
skinned or by reason of its extreme impenetrability, but because its
history is lost.

The American Negro has changed his temper. Now he wants his freedom. Whether he is smiling at you or not, he wants his freedom.

Songs of liberation—who can lock them up? The spirit of free-dom—who can jail it? A people's unity—what lash can beat it down? Civil rights—what doubletalk can satisfy our need?

We ask for nothing that is not right, and herein lies the great power of our demand.

Neither the old-time slavery, nor continued prejudice need extin-guish self-respect, crush manly ambition or paralyze effort.

One of the great measures of a people is its culture, its artistic stature.

In my music, my plays, my films I want to carry always this central idea: to be African. Multitudes of men have died for less worthy ideals; it is even more eminently worth living for.

Having been given, I must give.

Yes, here is my homeground—here and in all the Negro communi-ties throughout the land. Here I stand.

Jackie Robinson

1919–1972 ◆ baseball player, TV sports analyst, businessman, and
activist/fundraiser for the NAACP ◆ the first African American
to break the color barrier in the major leagues when he was
recruited to play for the Brooklyn Dodgers in 1947
◆ first African American in the Baseball Hall of Fame
◆ autobiography, *I Never Had It Made*

My fight was against the barriers that kept Negroes out of baseball. This was the area where I found imperfection, and where I was able to fight. And I fought because I knew it was not doomed to be a losing fight.

I had to fight hard against loneliness, abuse, and the knowledge that any mistake I made would be magnified because I was the only black man out there. Many people resented my impatience and honesty, but I never cared about acceptance as much as I cared about respect.

At the beginning of the World Series of 1947, I experienced a completely new emotion when the National Anthem was played. This time, I thought, it is being played for me, as much as for anyone else.

Fear is a two-edged sword that sometimes cuts the wielder.

The many of us who attain what we may and forget those who help us along the line, we've got to remember that there are so many others to pull along the way. The farther they go, the further we all go.

Baseball is like a poker game. Nobody wants to quit when he's losing; nobody wants you to quit when you're ahead.

[*on his retirement*] Athletes die twice.

Chris Rock

Born 1965 ◆ comedian, writer, actor, film producer and director, and TV personality ◆ films include *CB4, Beverly Hills Ninja, Down to Earth*, and *Death at a Funeral* ◆ TV credits include *Saturday Night Live, In Living Color*, and *The Chris Rock Show* ◆ quasi-autobiography, *Rock This!*

A man is only as faithful as his options.

I don't get high, but sometimes I wish I did. That way, when I messed up in life I would have an excuse. But right now there's no rehab for stupidity.

Every town has two malls: the one white people go to and the one white people used to go to.

Much like rock 'n' roll, school shootings were invented by the black man and stolen by the whites.

Yeah, I love being famous. It's almost like being white, y'know?

J. A. Rogers

1880–1966 ◆ writer, reporter, and historian ◆ Harlem Renaissance notable ◆ pioneer in the field of black studies ◆ books include *From Superman to Man, Sex and Race*, and *Africa's Gift to America*

The Negro has a field all to himself in musical expression. His enemies will listen to his music when they will hear nothing else.

The worship of the black woman as the mother of the human race goes back to the dimmest antiquity.

Jazz isn't music merely, it is a spirit that can express itself in almost anything. The true spirit of jazz is a joyous revolt from convention, custom, authority, boredom, even sorrow—from everything that would confine the soul of man and hinder its riding free on the air.

Diana Ross

Born 1944 ◆ singer, film and TV actress, and entrepreneur ◆ lead
singer of The Supremes ◆ films include *Lady Sings the Blues*,
Mahogany, and *The Wiz* ◆ autobiography, *Secrets of a Sparrow*

I have found thoughts and words to be the foundation for success and failure in life. I'm teaching my kids when to whisper and when to shout.

I really, deeply believe that dreams do come true. Often, they might not come true when you want them. They come in their own time.

I'm not really a songwriter—I'm an interpreter. So in a sense I am an actress first and foremost. I act out the songs, and I lead with my heart.

I never considered it to be a disadvantage to be a black woman. I never wanted to be anything else. We have brains! We're beautiful! We should be able to do anything we set our minds to!

I think a responsibility comes with notoriety, but I never think of it as power.

I was lucky, and if I have any bad memories, I hope they're not true.

Carl T. Rowan

1925–2000 ◆ journalist and government official ◆ one of the first
African-American naval officers of World War II ◆ director of the
United States Information Agency ◆ nationally syndicated
columnist ◆ political commentator on radio and TV ◆ memoir,
Breaking Barriers

A society is never more in peril than when the people lose the ability to identify a genuine threat to personal liberty.

It is often easier to become outraged by injustice half a world away than by oppression and discrimination half a block from home.

The library is the temple of learning, and learning has liberated more people than all the wars in history.

A minority group has "arrived" only when it has the right to produce some fools and scoundrels without the entire group paying for it.

Nothing wilts faster than laurels that have been rested upon.

You gotta get tired before you retire.

Wilma Rudolph

1940–1994 ◆ track and field athlete ◆ the first American to win three gold medals in a single Olympics ◆ founder of the Wilma Rudolph Foundation to promote amateur athletics ◆ Black Athletes Hall of Fame and National Track and Field Hall of Fame ◆ autobiography, *Wilma*

My doctors told me I would never walk again. My mother told me I would. I believed my mother.

I ran and ran and ran every day, and I acquired this sense of determination, this sense of spirit that I would never, never give up, no matter what else happened.

I grew up in a small, segregated southern town, but the oppression there was nothing compared to the oppression I saw in the big-city black ghetto.

The reward is not so great without the struggle.

Never underestimate the power of dreams and the influence of the human spirit. We are all the same in this notion: The potential for greatness lives within each of us.

It doesn't matter what you're trying to accomplish. It's all a matter of discipline.

No matter what accomplishments you make, somebody helps you.

Winning is great, sure, but if you are really going to do something in life, the secret is learning how to lose. Nobody goes undefeated all the time. If you can pick up after a crushing defeat, and go on to win again, you are going to be a champion someday.

RuPaul

Born 1960 ◆ a.k.a. RuPaul Andre Charles ◆ entertainer, model,
singer, actor, dancer, cable TV host, and drag queen ◆ pop culture
icon ◆ films include *The Brady Bunch Movie* and *Crooklyn*
◆ albums include *Red Hot* and *Champion* ◆ autobiography,
Lettin' It All Hang Out

Everybody say "Love"!

With hair, heels, and attitude, honey, I am through the roof.

All sins are forgiven once you start making a lot of money.

At five years old, I realized I was a superstar trapped in a five-year-old's body. And I had to do something about that.

I don't have to explain myself. My frequency is very common and is open to anybody who wants to tune in.

Look at me—a big old black man under all of this makeup, and if I can look beautiful, so can you.

If you don't love yourself, how in the hell you gonna love somebody else?

We're born naked and the rest is drag.

Bayard Rustin

1910–1987 ◆ writer, civil rights leader, advocate for nonviolent
resistance, and singer ◆ helped organize the NY branch of CORE,
as well as the SCLC ◆ books include *Which Way Out? A Way Out
of the Exploding Ghetto* and *Time on Two Crosses:
The Collected Writings of Bayard Rustin*

To engage in anti-Semitism is to engage in self-destruction.

When an individual is protesting society's refusal to acknowledge his dignity as a human being, his very act of protest confers dignity on him.

Who are the nonvoters? By and large, they are poor and low-income people who get the worst deal in this society. On the other hand, those who vote generally have higher incomes and better educations. They get the best deal—which is why they vote. They have their stake and they mean to keep it.

There is a strong moralistic strain in the civil rights movement that would remind us that power corrupts, forgetting that the absence of power also corrupts.

Blacks are no longer the litmus paper of the barometer of social change. . . . The new "niggers" are gays. . . . The question of social change should be framed with the most vulnerable group in mind: gay people.

Sonia Sanchez

Born 1934 ◆ poet, writer, playwright, educator, and scholar
◆ closely associated with the Black Arts Movement ◆ American
Book Award winner for *Homegirls and Handgrenades* ◆ other books
include *Morning Haiku* and *Does Your House Have Lions?*

Poetry is a subconscious conversation, it is as much the work of those who understand it as those who make it.

Art, no matter what its intention, reacts to or reflects the culture it springs from.

The most fundamental truth to be told in any art form, as far as blacks are concerned, is that America is killing us. But we continue to live and love and struggle and win.

So much of growing up is an unbearable waiting. A constant longing for another time. Another season.

I keep writing because I realize that until black people's social reality is free of oppression and exploitation, I will not be free to write as one who's not oppressed or exploited. That is the goal. That is the struggle and the dream.

I cannot tell the truth about anything unless I confess being a student, growing and learning something new every day. The more I learn, the clearer my view of the world becomes.

The best way to live in this world is to live above it.

Arthur A. Schomburg

1874–1938 ◆ historian, writer, and social activist ◆ Harlem
Renaissance notable and archivist whose extensive collection of
artifacts and works of African-American history and art became the
basis for the Schomburg Center for Research in Black Culture at
the New York Public Library branch in Harlem

The American Negro must remake his past in order to make his
future. Though it is orthodox to think of America as the one country
where it is unnecessary to have a past, what is a luxury for the nation
as a whole becomes a prime social necessity for the Negro.

History must restore what slavery took away, for it is the social
damage of slavery that the present generations must repair and
offset.

By virtue of their being regarded as something "exceptional," even
by friends and well-wishers, Negroes of attainment and genius have
been unfairly disassociated from the group, and group credit lost
accordingly.

Just as black men were influential factors in the campaign against
the slave trade, so they were among the earliest instigators of the
abolition movement.

The bigotry of civilization which is the taproot of intellectual prejudice begins far back and must be corrected at its source.
Fundamentally it has come about from that depreciation of Africa
which has sprung up from ignorance of her true role and position in
human history and the early development of culture.

Among the rising democratic millions we find the Negro thinking
more collectively, more retrospectively than the rest, and apt out of
the very pressure of the present to become the most enthusiastic
antiquarian of them all.

It is the season to devote our time to kindling the torch that will
inspire us to racial integrity.

Hazel Scott

1920–1981 ◆ jazz and classical pianist, songwriter, actress, recording artist, civil rights activist, and feminist ◆ first African-American woman to have her own TV show ◆ performed at Carnegie Hall ◆ target of the House Un-American Activities Committee (HUAC) during the McCarthy era

I've always known I was gifted, which is not the easiest thing in the world for a person to know, because you're not responsible for your gift, only for what you do with it.

I think integration is greatly overrated. I don't think there is any such thing as integration, because you can't integrate a person's mind.

It's not just in the United States but all through the Western Hemisphere that you get the black man's art form, which is the beat of Africa.

I have always respected everyone's religion. . . . [T]here is only one God and a lot of confused people.

There's only one free person in this society, and he is white and male.

There's a time when you have to explain to your children why they're born, and it's a marvelous thing if you know the reason by then.

Any woman who has a great deal to offer the world is in trouble. And if she's a black woman, she's in deep trouble.

Bobby Seale

Born 1936 ◆ author, lecturer, and radical civil rights activist ◆ co-founder and chairman of the Black Panther Party ◆ books include *Seize the Time* and his autobiography, *A Lonely Rage*

We don't hate nobody because of their color. We hate oppression!

You don't fight racism with racism, the best way to fight racism is with solidarity.

The enslavement of black people from the very beginning of this country, the genocide practiced on the American Indians and the confining of the survivors on reservations, the savage lynching of thousands of black men and women, the dropping of atomic bombs on Hiroshima and Nagasaki, and . . . the cowardly massacre in Vietnam, all testify to the fact that toward people of color the racist power structure of America has but one policy: repression, genocide, terror, and the big stick.

Tupac Shakur

Born 1971–1996 ◆ poet, rapper, actor, and civil rights activist ◆ bestselling rap artist worldwide ◆ hits include "California Love" and "Dear Mama" ◆ films include *Juice* and *Poetic Justice* ◆ book of poetry, *The Rose that Grew from Concrete*

If we really are saying rap is an art form, then we got to be true to it and be more responsible for our lyrics. If you see everybody dying because of what you're saying, it don't matter that you didn't make them die, it just matters that you didn't save them.

Life's a wheel of fortune and it's my chance to spin it.

The only thing that comes to a sleeping man is dreams.

I am society's child, this is how they made me, and now I'm sayin' what's on my mind and they don't want that. This is what you made me, America.

Let me say for the record, I am not a gangster and never have been. I'm not the thief who grabs your purse. I'm not the guy who jacks your car. I'm not down with the people who steal and hurt others. I'm just a brother who fights back.

I don't have no fear of death. My only fear is coming back reincarnated.

Before you can understand what I mean, you have to know how I lived or how the people I'm talking to live.

Al Sharpton, Jr.

Born 1954 ◆ minister, orator, civil rights leader, social activist, and radio talk show host ◆ tour manager for soul singer, James Brown ◆ founder of the National Action Network and the National Youth Movement ◆ autobiography, *Go and Tell Pharaoh*

We have defeated Jim Crow, but now we have to deal with his son, James Crow Jr., esquire.

I come from a base of angry people who need me to articulate their grievances.

If the poor can be scapegoated today, who can be tomorrow? It's as though it's somehow criminal to be unfortunate. Over sixty percent of the children who are classified as poor in this country are the children of people who work every day. This is a battle for the soul of this country. A battle between the Christian right and the right Christians.

I've seen enough things to know that if you just keep on going, if you turn the corner, the sun will be shining.

If Charlton Heston can have a constitutional right to carry a rifle, why can't grandma have a constitutional right to health care.

My ministry's always been one of social activism. I think a responsible minister must be at some levels involved in the social order.

All politicians have baggage. It's just that some politicians get skycaps to carry their baggage. I have to carry my own.

I was raised by a single mother who made a way for me. She used to scrub floors as a domestic worker, put a cleaning rag in her pocket book and ride the subways in Brooklyn so I would have food on the table. But she taught me . . . that life is about not where you start, but where you're going. That's family values.

We're not anti-police . . . we're anti-police brutality.

If I use the media, even with tricks, to publicize a black youth being shot in the back . . . then I should be praised for it; and it's more of a comment on them than me that it would take tricks to make them cover the loss of life.

I am a watchman. I've been designated to stand on the wall and tell what I see.

Russell Simmons

Born 1957 ◆ entrepreneur, producer, social activist, and
philanthropist ◆ co-founder of the pioneering rap label Def Jam
Recordings and founder of Rush Communications ◆ Broadway
show *Def Poetry* and HBO series *Def Comedy Jam*
◆ autobiography, *Life and Def: Sex, Drugs, Money, + God*

I'm not a politician. I only want to help relieve the suffering in communities, and I want to help people see their community in each other.

If you learn late, you pass it on to people so they can learn early.

Hip-hop has . . . changed the world. It has taken something from the
American ghetto and made it global. It has become the creative touch-
stone for edgy, progressive and aggressive youth culture around the
world.

Rappers want to change the world to suit their vision and to create a
place for themselves in it. So kids can find a way into hip-hop by
staying true to their instinct toward rebellion and change.

[Rap is] the last step of the civil rights movement. You know, wrap
your hands around some money.

Nina Simone

1933–2003 ◆ "High Priestess of Soul" ◆ singer, songwriter, pianist,
and civil rights activist ◆ CORE designated her song, "To Be
Young, Gifted, and Black," the black national anthem
◆ autobiography, *I Put a Spell on You*

Music is a gift and a burden I've had since I can remember who I
was. I was born into music. The decision was how to make the best
use of it.

During the sixties my people started having riots and saying, we
want this and we want that. I said, well, okay, now I can change my
direction from love songs and things that are not related to what's
happening, to something that is happening for my people.

Jazz is not music, it's a way of life, it's a way of being, a way of
thinking. I think that the Negro in America is jazz. Everything he
does—the slang he uses, the way he walks, the way he talks, his
jargon, the new inventive phrases we make up to describe things—all
that to me is jazz just as much as the music we play.

Charlie Parker and Billie Holiday are our father and mother.

How do you explain what it feels like to get on the stage and make poetry that you know sinks into the hearts and souls of people who are unable to express it?

John Singleton

Born 1968 ◆ screenwriter, film producer and director ◆ first African American nominated for an Oscar for Best Director, and the youngest, at age twenty-four ◆ films include *Boyz N the Hood* and *Rosewood*

A whole generation doesn't respect themselves, which makes it easier for them to shoot each other. This is a generation of kids who don't have father figures. They're looking for their manhood, and they get a gun.

Ever since black people were brought here—dragged, kicking and screaming, out of the motherland—we've been under some police state, whether it's slavery or the LAPD.

[on his film Rosewood*]* Ours is a morbid history; most try to evade it. Black people don't want to remember being victims of lynching, rape, the separation of families, living under Jim Crow and all the other horrors those things entailed. And white folk don't want to remember being the perpetrators of that kind of persecution.

Gangs are just a symptom of the problems in the black community. They're a rite of passage to manhood. Every society has that. For black youths in South Central [LA], it's joining a gang. In another society, it's joining a football team. The problem with the rite of passage in South Central is that it can get you killed.

Sister Souljah

Born 1964 ◆ née Lisa Williamson ◆ writer, rap musician, feminist, social activist, and public speaker ◆ founder of the African Youth Survival Camp ◆ executive director of Daddy's House Social Programs, Inc., for urban youth ◆ books include *The Coldest Winter Ever*, and her memoir, *No Disrespect*

I'm inclined to remind people of the things they'd most like to forget.

Anger cancels good judgment.

Rap music is powerful because it puts people in leadership who would not ordinarily be allowed to speak, rap, rhyme, sing or say anything.

Mothers . . . are the narrators of your life. They either tell you a good story or a bad story or a balanced story.

A person who is arrogant is also ignorant.

America still has a lot of unspoken racial laws. Saying what you think if you're black is still considered uppity.

It is possible . . . to be academically advanced and culturally retarded.

[Harriet Tubman is] the strongest person in the history of African people in this country. She was an activist. She took action. She was a soldier. She was a warrior.

You can't call me or any black person any place in the world a racist. We don't have the power to do to white people, what white people have done to us. And even if we did, we don't have that low down dirty nature.

What I am is natural and serious and as sensitive as an open nerve on an ice cube. I'm a young black sister with an unselfish heart who overdosed on love long ago.

Shelby Steele

Born 1946 ◆ writer, journalist, and educator ◆ books include
The Content of Our Character: A New Vision of Race in America
(winner of the National Book Critics' Circle Award) and *White Guilt: How Blacks and Whites Together Destroyed the Promise of the Civil Rights Era*

What both black and white Americans fear are the sacrifices and risks that true racial harmony demands. This fear is the measure of our racial chasm.

Being "black" in no way spared me the necessity of being myself.

The great ingenuity of interventions like affirmative action has not been that they give Americans a way to identify with the struggle of blacks, but that they give them a way to identify with racial virtuousness quite apart from blacks.

The promised land guarantees nothing. It is only an opportunity, not a deliverance.

Opportunity follows struggle. It follows effort. It follows hard work. It doesn't come before.

I am strained to defend racial quotas and any affirmative action that supersedes merit.

Personal responsibility is the brick and mortar of power.

Clifton L. Taulbert

Born 1945 ◆ writer, educator, and speaker ◆ autobiographical trilogy, *Once Upon a Time When We Were Colored, The Last Train North*, and *Watching Our Crops Come In* ◆ children's books include the *Little Cliff* series

Man cannot really own the land; we are only trustees for a time. Eventually the land will claim us and we'll return to our mother earth.

As a child, I was not only protected, but also nourished, encouraged, taught, and loved by people who, with no land, little money and few other resources, displayed the strength of a love which knew no measure. I have come to believe that this love is the true value, the legitimate measure of a people's worth.

Today my children are growing up in a world where "color" is something that comes in a box of crayons.

It was closer to our hearts than our homes—the colored church. It was more than an institution, it was the very heartbeat of our lives. Our church was all our own, beyond the influence of whites, with its own societal structure.

Field hands were deacons, and maids were ushers, mothers of the church, or trustees. The church transformed the ordinary into an institution of social and economic significance. A hard week of field work forgotten, the maid's aprons laid to rest, and the tractors in the shed, these colored men and women had entered a world that was all their own.

Susan L. Taylor

Born 1946 ✦ writer and editor ✦ founder and CEO, National
CARES Mentoring Movement ✦ editor-in-chief emeritus of
Essence magazine ✦ books include *In the Spirit* and
Lessons in Living

In every crisis there is a message. Crises are nature's way of forcing change—breaking down old structures, shaking loose negative habits so that something new and better can take their place.

Whatever we believe about ourselves and our ability comes true for us.

Use missteps as stepping stones to deeper understanding and greater achievement.

Self-hate is a form of mental slavery that results in poverty, ignorance and crime.

Each moment is magical, precious and complete and will never come again.

The most sacred place isn't the church, the mosque, or the temple, it's the temple of the body. That's where spirit lives.

Our greatest problems in life come not so much from situations we confront as from our doubts about our ability to handle them.

Faith is the flip side of fear.

We are the first generation of black people in four hundred years who can live our dreams.

Mary Church Terrell

1863–1954 ✦ civil rights activist, women's suffrage advocate, writer,
lecturer, and educator ✦ founding member of the NAACP
✦ founder and president of the National Association of Colored
Women ✦ autobiography, *A Colored Woman in a White World*

Stop using the word "Negro." . . . It does not represent a country or anything else except one single, solitary color. . . . We are the only human beings in the world with fifty-seven varieties of complexions who are classed together as a single racial unit. Therefore, we are really colored people and that is the only name in the English language which accurately describes us.

It is a great pity the word "Negro" was not outlawed in the Emancipation Proclamation. . . . After people have been freed, it is a cruel injustice to call them by the same name they bore as slaves.

It is impossible for any white person in the United States, no matter how sympathetic and broad, to realize what life would mean to him if his incentive to effort were suddenly snatched away. To the lack of incentive to effort, which is the awful shadow under which we live, may be traced the wreck and ruin of scores of colored youth.

When Ernestine Rose, Lucretia Mott, Elizabeth Cady Stanton, Lucy Stone and Susan B. Anthony began that agitation by which colleges were opened to women . . . colored women were not only refused admittance to institutions of learning but the law of the States in which the majority lived made it a crime to teach them to read.

A white woman has only one handicap to overcome, that of sex. I have two, both race and sex.

Clarence Thomas

Born 1948 ◆ attorney and judge ◆ legal counsel for Monsanto
◆ chairman of the Equal Employment Opportunity Commission
(EEOC) ◆ 106th Supreme Court justice ◆ memoir,
My Grandfather's Son

I am the product of hatred and love—the hatred of the social and political structure which dominated the segregated, hate-filled city of my youth, and the love of some people—my mother, my grandparents, my neighbors and relatives—who said by their actions, "You can make it, but first you must endure."

[on his confirmation hearings for Supreme Court justice in 1991]
[This] is a high-tech lynching for uppity blacks who in any way deign to think for themselves, to have different ideas, and it is a message that unless you kowtow to an old order, this is what will happen to you. You will be lynched, destroyed, caricatured by a committee of the U.S. Senate rather than hung from a tree.

Any discrimination, like sharp turns in a road, becomes critical because of the tremendous speed at which we are traveling into the high-tech world of a service economy.

I don't believe in quotas. America was founded on a philosophy of individual rights, not group rights.

Race-conscious remedies in this society are dangerous. You can't orchestrate society along racial lines or different lines by saying there should be ten percent blacks, fifteen percent Hispanics.

Howard Thurman

c. 1899–1981 ◆ poet, writer, minister, educator, and civil rights leader ◆ co-founder of the Church for the Fellowship of All Peoples, the first multiracial and nondenominational church in the U.S. ◆ books include *The Negro Spiritual Speaks of Life and Death*, and his autobiography, *With Head and Heart*

He who fears is literally delivered to destruction.

A man must be at home somewhere before he can feel at home everywhere.

It is the family that gives us a deep private sense of belonging. Here we first begin to have our self defined for us.

Love always sees more than is in evidence at any moment of viewing.

Not to fight at all is to choose a weapon by which one fights. Perhaps the authentic moral stature of a man is determined by his choice of weapons which he uses in his fight against the adversary. Of all weapons, love is the most deadly and devastating, and few there be who dare trust their fate in its hands.

If we are good to the child and to other people, he will get from us directly a conception of goodness more profound and significant than all the words we may use about goodness as an ideal.

One who has no sense of being an object of love is seriously handicapped in making someone else an object of love.

This is the first miracle, a man becomes his dreams; then it is that the line between what he does and is and his dream melts away.

When a man is despised and hated by other men and all around are the instruments of violence in behalf of such attitudes, then he may find himself resorting to hatred as a means of salvaging a sense of self, however fragmented.

There is something in every one of you that waits and listens for the sound of the genuine in yourself. It is the only true guide you will ever have. And if you cannot hear it, you will all of your life spend your days on the ends of strings that somebody else pulls.

Wallace Thurman

1902–1934 ◆ writer, dramatist, and literary critic ◆ *"enfant terrible"*
of the Harlem Renaissance ◆ best known for *The Blacker the Berry:*
A Novel of Negro Life

If but a few live coals are found in a mountain of ashes, no one
should be disappointed. Genius is a rare quality in this world, and
there is no reason why it should be more ubiquitous among blacks
than whites.

Color prejudice and religion are akin in one respect. Some folks
have it and some don't, and the kernel that is responsible for it is
present in us all.

All people seem subject to prejudice, even those who suffer from it
most, and all people seem inherently to dislike other folk who are
characterized by cultural and lingual differences. It is a failing of
man, a curse of humanity.

[on the Harlem Renaissance] We are journeymen, planting seeds
for someone else to harvest.

Mamie Till-Mobley

1921–2003 ◆ educator, lecturer, and civil rights activist ◆
mother of Emmett Till, whose murder helped spark the civil rights
movement ◆ memoir, *Death of Innocence:*
The Story of the Hate Crime That Changed America

Two months ago I had a nice apartment in Chicago. I had a good
job. I had a son. When something happened to the Negroes in the
South, I said, "That's their business, not mine." Now I know how
wrong I was. The murder of my son has shown me that what
happens to any of us, anywhere in the world, had better be the
business of us all.

IN MEMORIAM: EMMETT LOUIS TILL, 1941–1955: A little nobody who
shook up the world.

Melvin B. Tolson

1898–1966 ◆ poet, writer, playwright, columnist, and educator
◆ best known for his book, *"Harlem Gallery" and Other Poems*
◆ other books include *Caviar and Cabbage: Selected Columns*

Since we live in a changing universe, why do men oppose change? If a rock is in the way, the root of a tree will change its direction.

The New Negro breaks the icons of his detractors, wipes out the conspiracy of silence, speaks to *his* America.

Are you a poet first and then black; or are you black first and then a poet?

How could a civilization be "gone with the wind" unless there was something to MAKE it go?

It's easy to love God. It's easy to love Jesus. It's easy to pray for the heathen African ten thousand miles from the house where you live. It's hard to call a lousy tramp your brother and set him down at your table.

Jean Toomer

1894–1967 ◆ poet, writer, and playwright ◆ his collection of poetry
and sketches, *Cane*, is regarded as a landmark work of the
Harlem Renaissance ◆ other books include *The Wayward
and the Seeking: A Collection of Writings*

No eyes that have seen beauty ever lose their sight.

One may receive the information but miss the teaching.

Fear is a noose that binds until it strangles.

The realization of ignorance is the first act of knowing.

People mistake their limitations for high standards.

We have many reformers, few transformers.

In a sick world, it is the first duty of the artist to get well.

I feel that in time, in its social phase, my art will aid in giving the Negro to himself.

Robert Townsend

Born 1957 ◆ writer, actor, film director and producer ◆ creator of
the TV comedy series, *In Living Color* ◆ films include
Hollywood Shuffle, *The Five Heartbeats*, and *Phantom Punch*

He who controls images controls everything.

True leadership must be for the benefit of the followers, not the
enrichment of the leaders.

Consultants are people who borrow your watch and tell you what
time it is, and then walk off with the watch.

I'm in the best field to do what I need to do. If you shoot for the stars,
and hit the moon, it's okay. But, you've got to shoot for something.

Sojourner Truth

c. 1797–1883 ◆ a.k.a. Isabella Baumfree ◆ abolitionist, feminist,
and orator ◆ memoir, *The Narrative of Sojourner Truth*

That man over there says that women need to be helped into
carriages, and lifted over ditches, and to have the best place everywhere. Nobody ever helps me into carriages, or over mud puddles,
or gives me any best place! And ain't I a woman?

You asked me if I was of your race. I am proud to say that I am of
the same race that you are, I am colored, thank God for that. I have
not the curse of God upon me for enslaving human beings.

I shall make [Americans] understand that there is a debt to the
Negro people which they never can repay. At least, then, they must
make amends.

That little man in black there, he says women can't have as much
rights as men, because Christ wasn't a woman! Where did your
Christ come from? From God and a woman! Man had nothing to
do with Him.

When we get our rights we shall not have to come to you for money,
for then we shall have money enough in our own pockets.

I used to work in the fields and bind grain, keeping up with the
cradler, but men doing no more, got twice as much pay.

If my cup won't hold but a pint and yours holds a quart, wouldn't
you be mean not to let me have my little half-measure full?

I am glad to see that men are getting their rights, but I want women to get theirs, and while the water is stirring I will step into the pool.

Religion without humanity is a poor human stuff.

If the first woman God ever made was strong enough to turn the world upside down all alone, these women together ought to be able to turn it back, and get it right side up again!

I am not going to die. I'm going home like a shooting star.

Truth burns up error.

Harriet Tubman

c. 1820–1913 ◆ a.k.a. Ariminta Ross ◆ "Moses of Her People"
◆ ex-slave and abolitionist ◆ conductor on the Underground
Railroad, helping escaped slaves on their way north to freedom
◆ in the Civil War, she served the Union as a scout, spy, and nurse
◆ founded a home for aged and indigent ex-slaves

I had reasoned this out in my mind; there was two things I had a *right* to, liberty or death. If I could not have one, I would have the other; for no man should take me alive.

You go on or die. Dead niggers tell no tales.

[*from slavery to freedom*] I had crossed the line of which I had so long been dreaming. I was free; but there was no one to welcome me to the land of freedom, I was a stranger in a strange land.

I freed thousands of slaves. I could have freed thousands more, if they had known they were slaves.

On my underground railroad, I never ran my train off the track and I never lost a passenger.

Henry McNeal Turner

1834–1915 ◆ writer, bishop, and civil rights activist ◆ leading
exponent of the "Back to Africa" campaign ◆ traveling preacher for
the African Methodist Episcopal Church (AME) ◆ works include
The Genius and Theory of Methodist Polity

There is no manhood future in the United States for the Negro. He may eke out an existence for generations to come, but he can never be a man—full, symmetrical and undwarfed.

I believe that two or three millions of us should return to the land of our ancestors, and establish our own nation, civilization, laws, customs . . . What the black man needs is a country.

We have as much right biblically and otherwise to believe that God is a Negro as white people have to believe that God is a fine-looking, symmetrical, and ornamental white man.

Men are hung, shot and burnt by bands of murderers who are almost invariably represented as the most influential and respectable citizens in the community, while the evidences of guilt and horrible deeds charged upon the murdered victims comes from the mouth of the bloody handed wretches who perpetrate the murders.

The black man cannot protect a country, if the country doesn't protect him; and if, tomorrow, a war should arise, I would not raise a musket to defend a country where my manhood is denied.

The Fourth of July—memorable in the history of our nation as the great day of independence to its countryman—had no claim upon our sympathies. They made a flag and threw it to the heavens and bid it float forever; but every star in it was against us.

Nat Turner

1800–1831 ✦ writer, preacher, and slave who led a notorious slave insurrection in 1831 ✦ *The Confessions of Nat Turner* were written a few days before he was hanged

I had too much sense to be raised, and, if I was, I would never be of any service to anyone as a slave.

Remember that ours is not a war for robbery, or to satisfy our passions; it is a struggle for freedom.

Tina Turner

Born 1939 ✦ a.k.a. Anna Mae Bullock ✦ R&B singer and actress ✦ hits include "Proud Mary" and "River Deep, Mountain High" ✦ subject of the biopic, *What's Love Got to Do with It?* ✦ Rock and Roll Hall of Fame ✦ autobiography, *I, Tina: My Life Story*

I never said "Well, I don't have this and I don't have that." I said, "I don't have this *yet*, but I'm going to get it."

Sometimes you've got to let *everything* go—purge yourself. I did that. I had nothing, but I had my freedom. . . . [W]hatever is bringing you down, get rid of it. Because you'll find that when you're free, your true creativity, your true self comes out.

I was a victim; I don't dwell on it.

The real power behind whatever success I have now was something I found myself—something that's in all of us, I think, a little piece of God just waiting to be discovered.

Cicely Tyson

Born 1933 ◆ actress of stage, screen and TV ◆ co-founder of the
Dance Theater of Harlem ◆ films include *Sounder*,
The Autobiography of Miss Jane Pittman, and the TV miniseries,
Oldest Living Confederate Widow Tells All ◆ plays include
The Blacks, Cool World, and *God's Trombones*

I know that God did not put me on the face of this earth to bang on a typewriter for the rest of my life!

I'm a woman, and I'm black. I wait for roles—first, to be written for a woman, then, to be written for a black woman. And then, I have the audacity to be selective about the kinds of roles I play. I've really got three strikes against me.

This constant reminder by society that I am "different" because of the color of my skin, once I step outside of my door, is not my problem—it's theirs. I have never made it my problem and never will. I will die for my right to be human—just human.

Challenges make you discover things about yourself that you never really knew. They're what make the instrument stretch—what make you go beyond the norm.

Mike Tyson

Born 1966 ◆ "Iron Mike" and "Kid Dynamite" ◆ the youngest
boxer to win the title of world heavyweight champion, and the first
to hold all three major heavyweight championship titles (WBA,
WBC, and IBF) simultaneously ◆ subject of the film
documentary, *Tyson*

I'm a regular kid from the ghetto striving to do something positive with myself. I happen to fight well.

Experience is sometimes better than money.

Everyone has a plan till they get punched in the mouth.

It makes you want to cry to see old friends who failed to beat the trap into which they were born. I could so easily have become one of them. I was running wild and I was either going to end up locked away in prison, or dead.

Some people try to get you out of slavery for you to be their slave.

Real freedom is having nothing. I was freer when I didn't have a cent.

I'm a dreamer. I have to dream and reach for the stars, and if I miss a star then I grab a handful of clouds.

Sarah Vaughan

1924–1990 ◆ "The Divine One" ◆ jazz singer and pianist
◆ winner of a Grammy Award for lifetime achievement and an
Emmy Award for individual achievement ◆ hits include "Body and
Soul," "How Long Has This Been Going On," and
"Send in the Clowns"

I am not a special person. I am a regular person who does special things.

I'd like to go broke again, and this time I'd like to spend all the money myself.

I can put the blues in whatever I sing.

I don't go for that star stuff. All the stars are in heaven.

Alice Walker

Born 1944 ◆ poet, writer, educator, and womanist ◆ author
of *The Color Purple*, winner of the Pulitzer Prize and the
National Book Award ◆ other books include *In Love and Trouble:
Stories of Black Women*, and *Horses Make a Landscape Look
More Beautiful*

In our particular society, it is the narrowed and narrowing view of life that often wins.

No person is your friend who demands your silence, or denies your right to grow.

Ignorance, arrogance, and racism have bloomed as Superior Knowledge in all too many universities.

The quietly pacifist peaceful always die to make room for men who shout.

Guided by my heritage of a love of beauty and a respect for strength—in search of my mother's garden I found my own.

I could never live happily in Africa—or anywhere else—until I could live freely in Mississippi.

The most common way people give up their power is by thinking they don't have any.

Life is better than death, I believe, if only because it is less boring, and because it has fresh peaches in it.

What the mind doesn't understand, it worships or fears.

Tea to the English is really a picnic indoors.

The most important question in the world is, "Why is the child crying?"

People do not wish to appear foolish; to avoid the appearance of foolishness, they are willing to remain actually fools.

The animals of the world exist for their own reasons. They were not made for humans any more than black people were made for white, or women created for men.

Civil Rights is a term that did not evolve out of black culture, but rather, out of American law. As such, it is a term of limitation.

We must cherish our old men. We must revere their wisdom, appreciate their insight, love the humanity of their words.

Black women were always imitating Harriet Tubman—escaping to become something unheard of.

Is there no place in a revolution for a person who *cannot* kill?

I try to teach my heart not to want things it can't have.

I believe in the soul. Furthermore, I believe it is prompt accountability for one's choices, a willing acceptance of responsibility for one's thoughts, behavior, and actions that make it powerful.

She look like she ain't long for this world but dressed well for the next.

Any God I ever felt in church I brought in with me.

White folks is a miracle of affliction.

Expect nothing. Live frugally on surprise.

Abortion, for many women, is more than an experience of suffering beyond anything most men will ever know, it is an act of mercy, and an act of self-defense.

Anybody can observe the Sabbath, but making it holy surely takes the rest of the week.

The artist is the voice of the people.

I have learned not to worry about love; but to honor its coming with all my heart.

I think it pisses God off if you walk by the color purple in a field somewhere and don't notice it.

Madame C. J. Walker

1867–1919 ◆ a.k.a. Sarah Breedlove ◆ cosmetics entrepreneur, civil rights activist, and philanthropist ◆ first African-American woman to become a self-made millionaire ◆ National Women's Hall of Fame

America doesn't respect anything but money. . . . What our people need is a few millionaires.

I am a woman who came from the cotton fields of the South. I was promoted from there to the washtub. Then I was promoted to the cook kitchen, and from there I promoted myself into the business of manufacturing hair goods and preparations.

I had to make my own living and my own opportunity. . . . Don't sit down and wait for the opportunities to come; you have to get up and make them.

It's pretty hard for the Lord to guide you if you haven't made up your mind which way you want to go.

I got myself a start by giving myself a start.

THE SECRET OF A HAPPY LIFE: Lord help me live from day to day in such a self-forgotten way that when I kneel to pray my prayer shall be for—OTHERS.

David Walker

1785–1830 ♦ writer, militant abolitionist, orator, and merchant
♦ writer for *Freedom's Journal*, a black antislavery publication
♦ author of *David Walker's Appeal to the Coloured Citizens
of the World*

They think because they hold us in their infernal chains of slavery, that we wish to be white, or of their color—but they are dreadfully deceived—we wish to be just as it pleased our Creator to have made us.

The greatest riches in all America have arisen from our blood and tears.

God will not suffer us always to be oppressed. Our sufferings will come to an *end*, in spite of all the Americans, this side of *eternity*.

The bare name of educating the coloured people, scares our cruel oppressors almost to death.

If you commence, make sure you work—do not trifle, for they will not trifle with you—they want us for their slaves and think nothing of murdering us in order to subject us to that wretched condition—therefore, if there is an *attempt* made by us, kill or be killed.

I ask you, had you not rather be killed than be a slave to a tyrant, who takes the life of your mother, wife, and dear little children?

Treat us like men, and there is no danger but we will all live in peace and happiness together. For we are not like you, hard-hearted, unmerciful, and unforgiving.

Margaret Walker

1915–1998 ♦ poet, writer, educator, and lecturer ♦ founder of the
Margaret Walker Alexander National Research Center ♦ books
include *Jubilee, This Is My Century: New and Collected Poems*, and
Richard Wright: Daemonic Genius

Our children . . . do not allow us to remain cowards, complacent, nor withdrawn. They force us to face the bitterness and dare us to explain the pain. Much as it hurts, we owe them the truth.

There were bizarre beginnings in old lands for the making of me.

Talk had feet and could walk, and gossip had wings and could fly.

Love stretches your heart and makes you big inside.

The poetry of a people comes from the deep recesses of the uncon-
scious, the irrational, and the collective body of our ancestral
memories.

Fats Waller

1904–1943 ◆ singer, musician, composer, and bandleader
◆ instruments included "stride" piano and organ ◆ co-wrote
scores for Broadway shows *Hot Chocolates*, *Keep Shufflin'*, and
Load of Coal ◆ hits include "Honeysuckle Rose" and
"Ain't Misbehavin' "

One never know, do one?

They stopped me from swinging in church, so I had to swing outside.

I'm very glad to see that jazz has finally come back to his pappy,
Melody. . . . [T]he thing that makes a tune click is the melody, and
give the public four bars of that to dig their teeth into, and you have
a killer-diller.

"Ain't Misbehavin' " was written while I was lodged in the alimony
jail, and I wasn't misbehaving, you dig?

I'd like to close with a message to my dear little wife—get that man
outta there, honey, 'cause I'm coming home directly.

Samuel Ringgold Ward

1817–1866 ◆ writer, abolitionist, pastor, educator, orator, and
newspaper owner-editor ◆ conductor on the Underground Railroad
◆ raised funds for the Antislavery Society of Canada which helped
escaped slaves from the U.S. ◆ books include
Autobiography of a Fugitive Negro

As a black man, my labors will be antislavery labors.

Among the heaviest of my maledictions against slavery is that which
it deserves for keeping my poor father—and many like him—in the
midnight and dungeon of the grossest ignorance.

There are many attempts to get up compromises—and there is no term which I detest more than this, it is always the term which makes right yield to wrong; it has always been accursed since Eve made the first compromise with the devil.

I was born a slave—where? Wherever it was, it was where I dare not be seen or known, lest those who held my parents and ancestors in slavery should make a claim, hereditary or legal, in some form, to the ownership of my body and soul.

We who are slaveborn derive a comfort and solace from the death of those dearest to us, if they have the sad misfortune to be BLACKS and AMERICANS.

What an ever-present demon the spirit of hate is.

Booker T. Washington

1856–1915 ◆ writer, political leader, educator, and orator ◆
first president of the Tuskegee Institute ◆ books include
The Story of My Life and Work and *Up From Slavery*

No greater injury can be done to any youth than to let him feel that because he belongs to this or that race he will be advanced in life regardless of his own merits or efforts.

At the bottom of education, at the bottom of politics, even at the bottom of religion, there must be for our race economic independence.

The individual who can do something that the world wants done will, in the end, make his way regardless of his race.

Few are too young, and none too old, to make the attempt to learn.

To be successful, grow to the point where one completely forgets himself; that is, to lose himself in a great cause.

Nothing ever comes to one, that is worth having, except as a result of hard work.

You go to school, you study about the Germans and the French, but not about your own race. I hope the time will come when you study black history too.

Character, not circumstances, makes the man.

I think I have learned that the best way to lift one's self up is to help someone else.

Of all forms of slavery there is none that is so harmful and degrading as that form of slavery which tempts one human being to hate another by reason of his race or color. One man cannot hold another man down in the ditch without remaining down in the ditch with him.

I have learned that success is to be measured not so much by the position that one has reached in life as by the obstacles which he has overcome while trying to succeed.

I learned the lesson that great men cultivate love, and that only little men cherish a spirit of hatred.

I would permit no man, no matter what his color might be, to narrow and degrade my soul by making me hate him.

It seems to me that it is best to lay hold of the things we can put right rather than those we can do nothing but find fault with.

No race can prosper till it learns that there is as much dignity in tilling a field as in writing a poem. It is at the bottom of life we must begin, and not at the top. Nor should we permit our grievances to overshadow our opportunities.

In all things that are purely social we can be as separate as the fingers, yet one as the hand in all things essential to mutual progress.

Above all races and political boundaries there is humanity.

I am willing to be misjudged, if need be, if I can accomplish a little good.

When you meet an American Negro who's not Methodist or a Baptist, some white man's been tampering with his religion.

When a white boy undertakes a task, it is taken for granted that he will succeed. On the other hand, people are usually surprised if the Negro boy does not fail. In a word, the Negro youth starts out with the presumption against him.

There was never a time in my youth, no matter how dark and discouraging the days might be, when one resolve did not continually remain with me, and that was a determination to secure an education at any cost.

Success always leaves footprints.

Denzel Washington

Born 1954 ◆ actor, screenwriter, director, and producer ◆ Oscar
winner for Best Actor for his performance in *Training Day* and
winner (with his wife Pauletta) of the BET Humanitarian Award
◆ other films include *Malcolm X, The Hurricane, Remember the
Titans, A Soldier's Story,* and *Glory*

Acting is just a way of making a living. Family is life.

[I belong to] that minority among minorities—a working black
actor.

Where I think the most work needs to be done is behind the camera,
not in front of it.

I made a commitment to completely cut out drinking and anything
that might hamper me from getting my mind and body together.
And the floodgates of goodness have opened upon me—spiritually
and financially.

Luck is where opportunity meets preparation.

Fatherhood is responsibility, it's definitely humility, a lot of love and
the friendship of a parent and child.

My mother always told me, "Never give up because you never know
who's praying for you."

There are only four women in the world: the one you marry, your
mother, your daughter and all the rest of them. I tell men as long as
you keep that perspective, you'll be all right.

Harold Washington

1922–1987 ◆ lawyer, politician, orator, and civil rights activist
◆ member of Illinois State Legislature and the U.S. House of
Representatives ◆ first African-American mayor of Chicago

This is our country. We don't have to slip around like peons or
thieves in the middle of the night, asking someone for open sesame.
Knock the damn door down!

Most of our problems can be solved. Some of them will take brains,
and some of them will take patience, but all of them will have to be
wrestled with like an alligator in the swamp.

If there were an honest election in this city [Chicago], the whole country would go bananas.

As soon as we get control, the criticism becomes, "Oh, you just want to be another boss."

Black America has been the nation's conscience for two hundred years. It is time to help guide its conscious activities as well.

[his philosophy] "Do unto others." Be fair. It pays, not only as a moral imperative. I think it's common sense.

[on being elected the first black mayor of Chicago] We never stopped believing that we were part of something good that has never happened before.

Ethel Waters

1896–1977 ◆ blues and jazz vocalist, actress of stage, film, and TV ◆ first African-American woman to star on Broadway ◆ films include *Cabin in the Sky* and *Member of the Wedding* ◆ autobiography, *His Eye Is on the Sparrow*

Ours is the truest dignity of man, the dignity of the undefeated.

I was a tough child. I was too large and too poor to fit, and I fought back.

When I was a honky-tonk entertainer, I used to work from nine until unconsciousness. I was just a young girl, and when I tried to sing anything but the double-meaning songs, they'd say, "Oh, my God, Ethel, get hot!"

I have no acting technique, I act instinctively. That's why I can't play any role that isn't based on something in my life.

Asking what I considered an impossible salary when I didn't want to work for someone has boosted my pay again and again.

All the men in my life have been two things. an epic and an epidemic.

I ask the Lord for so much that I guess I keep him scufflin'.

It has been an ache and a joy both to look over this big shoulder of mine at all my yesterdays.

Ida B. Wells

1862–1931 ◆ educator, civil rights leader, women's rights advocate,
orator, journalist, and newspaper owner-editor ◆ documented
lynching and lynch law in the U.S. in *The Red Record* and
Southern Horrors ◆ autobiography, *Crusade for Justice*

Our country's national crime is *lynching*. It is not the creature of an hour, the sudden outburst of uncontrolled fury, or the unspeakable brutality of an insane mob. It represents the cool, calculating deliberation of intelligent people who openly avow that there is an "unwritten law" that justifies them in putting human beings to death without complaint under oath, without trial by jury, without opportunity to make defense, and without right of appeal.

It becomes the painful duty of the Negro to reproduce a record which shows that a large portion of the American people avow anarchy, condone murder, and defy the contempt of civilization.

In slave times the Negro was kept subservient and submissive by the frequency and severity of the scourging, but, with freedom, a new system of intimidation came in vogue; the Negro was not only whipped and scourged; he was killed.

Nowhere in the civilized world, save the United States, do men go out in bands, to hunt down, shoot, hang to death, a single individual.

Nobody in this section of the country believes the old threadbare lie that Negro men rape white women. If Southern white men are not careful, they will overreach themselves and public sentiment will have a reaction; a conclusion will then be reached which will be very damaging to the moral reputation of their women.

What becomes a crime deserving capital punishment when the tables are turned is a matter of small moment when the Negro woman is the accusing party.

True chivalry respects all womanhood, and no one who reads the record, as it is written in the faces of the million mulattoes in the South, will for a minute conceive that the southern white man had a very chivalrous regard for the honor due the women of his own race or respect for the womanhood which circumstances placed in his power.

The appeal to the white man's pocket has ever been more effectual than all the appeals ever made to his conscience.

Cornel West

Born 1953 ♦ writer, philosopher, scholar, educator, minister, orator, and social activist ♦ books include *Race Matters* and *Restoring Hope* ♦ memoir, *Brother West: Living and Loving Out Loud*

The black encounter with the absurd in racist American society yields a profound spiritual need for human affirmation and recognition. Hence, the centrality of religion and music—those most spiritual of human activities—in black life.

Let us hope and pray that the vast intelligence, imagination, humor, and courage of Americans will not fail us. Either we learn a new language of empathy and compassion, or the fire this time will consume us all.

The major enemy of black survival in America has been and is neither oppression nor exploitation but rather the nihilistic threat—that is, loss of hope and absence of meaning.

You can't lead the people if you don't love the people. You can't save the people if you don't serve the people.

The major form of evil in America civilization is white supremacy.

I understand the vocation of the intellectual as trying to turn easy answers into critical questions and ask these critical questions to those with power.

Humility is the fruit of inner security and wise maturity.

Market moralities and mentalities—fueled by economic imperatives to make a profit at nearly any cost—yield unprecedented levels of loneliness, isolation, and sadness. And our public life lies in shambles, shot through with icy cynicism and paralyzing pessimism.

It is impossible to grow up in America, no matter what color you are, and not have some white supremacy in you.

America—this monument to the genius of ordinary men and women, this place where hope becomes capacity, this long, halting turn of no into the yes—needs citizens who love it enough to reimagine and remake it.

To live is to wrestle with despair yet never to allow despair to have the last word.

Phillis Wheatley

1753–c. 1784 ◆ writer and poet ◆ a former slave, she was
the first published African-American poet with *Poems on
Various Subjects, Religious and Moral* ◆ other books include
The Memoirs and Poems of Phillis Wheatley and
The Letters of Phillis Wheatley

The world is a severe schoolmaster, for its frowns are less dang'rous than its smiles and flatteries, and it is a difficult task to keep in the path of Wisdom.

In every human breast, God has implanted a principle which we call love of freedom; it is impatient of oppression, and pants for deliverance.

Wisdom is higher than a fool can reach.

Walter F. White

1893–1955 ◆ writer, essayist, and civil rights leader ◆ Harlem
Renaissance notable ◆ executive secretary of the NAACP ◆ social
activist whose books include a study of lynching, *Rope and Faggot*
◆ autobiography, *A Man Called White*

Intolerance can grow only in the soil of ignorance: from its branches grow all manner of obstacles to human progress.

In any American village, North or South, East or West, there is no problem which cannot be solved in half an hour by the morons who lounge about the village store.

Lynching and mob violence, disenfranchisement, unequal distribution of school funds, the Ku Klux Klan and all other forms of racial prejudice are for one great purpose—that of keeping the Negro in the position where he is economically exploitable.

There is magic in a white skin; there is tragedy, loneliness, exile, in a black skin.

Either we must attain freedom for the whole world or there will be no world left for any of us.

John Edgar Wideman

Born 1941 ◆ writer, social critic, and educator ◆ his novel, *Sent for You Yesterday*, won the PEN/Faulkner Award, as did another novel, *Philadelphia Fire* ◆ memoirs, *Brothers and Keepers* and *Fatheralong: A Meditation on Fathers and Sons*

Color can be a cage and color consciousness can be terminal.

When I write I want to show how simple acts, simple words can be transformed to release their spiritual force. . . . I want to trace the comings and goings of my people on the invisible plane of existence where so much of the substance of black life resides.

He publishes one book—the text of suffering—over and over again. He disguises it between new boards, in different shapes and sizes, prints on varying papers, in many fonts, adds prefaces and postscripts to deceive the buyer, but it's always the same book.

The strong survive. The ones who are strong and *lucky*.

If you're born in black America you must quickly teach yourself to recognize the invisible barriers disciplining the space in which you may move.

Prison time must be hard time, a metaphorical death, a sustained, twilight, condition of death-in-life. The prisoner's life is violently interrupted, enclosed within a parenthesis. The point is to create the fiction that he doesn't exist. Prison is an experience of death by inches, minutes, hours, days.

The streets had been my stomping ground, my briar patch. The place I'd fled from with all my might, the place always snatching me back.

Every step and the way you take it here on enemy ground is a lesson.

Ralph Wiley

1952–2004 ◆ sports journalist and author ◆ writer for *Sports Illustrated* and ESPN.COM ◆ books include *Serenity: A Boxing Memoir* and *Why Black People Tend to Shout: Cold Facts and Wry Views from a Black Man's World*

It is not enviable to be feared, but it is preferable to being lynched.

Nothing captures the imagination like a guy with a big punch.

Since when did learning at school become "acting white"? Why isn't robbing, stealing, drinking, carousing, and spreading illnesses considered "acting white"? . . . I'd rather have learning at school called "acting black."

Truth knows no color; it appeals to intelligence.

Roy Wilkins

1901–1981 ◆ journalist, editor, orator, and civil rights leader ◆ executive director of the NAACP during the civil rights era ◆ awarded the Presidential Medal of Freedom ◆ autobiography, *Standing Fast*

[*on the murder of Emmett Till, 1955*] It would appear that the state of Mississippi has decided to maintain white supremacy by murdering children.

In a free society the police must be accountable to the people.

Like an individual who cannot solve a cancer problem, an alcohol problem, or a drug problem by denying it, a nation cannot deal fundamentally with racism by denying its existence. White people don't like to talk about racism because it is ugly.

Color doesn't mean very much to little children, black or white. Only as they grow older and absorb the poisons from adults does color begin to blind them.

No black history becomes significant and meaningful unless it is taught in the context of world and national history. In its sealed-off black-studies centers, it will be simply another exercise in racial breastfeeding.

[I fought against] a deep, unreasoning, savagely cruel refusal by too many white people to accept a simple, inescapable truth—the only master race is the human race, and we are all, by the grace of God, members of it.

Muffle your rage. Get smart instead of muscular.

Serena Williams

Born 1981 ✦ tennis player, sports icon, entrepreneur, and philanthropist ✦ two-time Olympic gold medal winner ✦ autobiography, *On the Line*

If you can keep playing tennis when somebody is shooting a gun down the street, that's concentration.

Luck has nothing to do with it, because I have spent many, many hours, countless hours, on the court working for my one moment in time, not knowing when it would come.

I'm a perfectionist. I'm pretty much insatiable. I feel there's so many things I can improve on.

[on competing professionally against her sister Venus] Tennis is just a game, family is forever.

Venus Williams

Born 1980 ✦ tennis player, sports icon, entrepreneur, and philanthropist ✦ three-time Olympic gold medal winner

When you lose, you're more motivated. When you win, you fail to see your mistakes and probably no one can tell you anything.

I'd like to imagine that in order to beat me a person would have to play almost perfect tennis.

I don't come to tournaments to make friends, to go to parties, to hold conversations. I come to be the best.

For women of color, for my family, it's one dream coming true after another.

August Wilson

1945–2005 ◆ poet and playwright ◆ awarded two Pulitzer Prizes for
Drama ◆ plays include *The Piano Lesson, Fences,* and
Joe Turner's Come and Gone

All you need in the world is love and laughter. That's all anybody
needs.

When you grab hold to a woman, you got something there. You got
a whole world there.

She's just using him to keep from being by herself. That's the worst
use of a man you can have.

It ain't nothing to find no starting place in the world. You just start
from where you find yourself.

There's no idea in the world that is not contained by black life. I
could write forever about the black experience in America.

Inside all blacks is one heartbeat that is fueled by the blood of
Africa.

You got to take the crooked with the straights.

Death ain't nothing but a fastball on the outside corner.

Style ain't nothing but keeping the same idea from beginning to
end. Everybody got it.

I might be a different kind of fool, but I ain't gonna be the same fool
twice.

I have always consciously been chasing the musicians. It's like our
culture is in the music. And the writers are way behind the musicians I see. So I'm trying to close the gap.

Freedom is heavy. You got to put your shoulder to freedom. Put
your shoulder to it and hope your back hold up.

Flip Wilson

1933–1998 ◆ comedian, actor, and TV personality ◆ best known
for *The Flip Wilson Show* ◆ winner of a Golden Globe and two
Emmy awards and a Grammy ◆ comedy albums include *The Devil
Made Me Buy This Dress* and *Cowboys and Colored People*

If you think nobody cares if you're alive, try missing a couple of car
payments.

The cost of living is going up and the chance of living is going down.

What you see is what you get!

The devil made me do it!

Violence is a tool of the ignorant.

You can't expect to hit the jackpot if you don't put a few nickels in the machine.

Oprah Winfrey

Born 1954 ◆ talk show host, actress, entrepreneur, and philanthropist ◆ founder of Oprah's Book Club, O: The Oprah Magazine, and her own production company, Harpo, Inc.

The more you praise and celebrate your life, the more there is in life to celebrate.

I'm black. I don't feel burdened by it and I don't think it's a huge responsibility. It's part of who I am. It does not define me.

For every one of us that succeeds, it's because there's somebody there to show you the way out. The light doesn't necessarily have to be in your family; for me it was teachers and school.

I was raised to believe that excellence is the best deterrent to racism or sexism. And that's how I operate my life.

I am where I am because of the bridges that I crossed. Sojourner Truth was a bridge. Harriet Tubman was a bridge. Ida B. Wells was a bridge. Madame C. J. Walker was a bridge. Fannie Lou Hamer was a bridge.

I've discovered if you treat people the way you wish to be treated at all times, you will get exactly what the universe has intended.

I'm a truth seeker. That's what I do every day on the show—put out the truth. Some people don't like it, they call it sensational, but I say life is sensational.

If you come to fame not understanding who you are, it will define who you are.

Failure is another stepping stone to greatness.

I still have my feet on the ground, I just wear better shoes.

You can have it all. You just can't have it all at one time.

George C. Wolfe

Born 1954 ◆ playwright, theater director and producer ◆ headed
the New York Shakespeare Festival ◆ directed
The Caucasian Chalk Circle and *Angels in America* ◆ plays
include *The Colored Museum, Jelly's Last Jam,* and *Spunk*

God created black people and black people created style.

We traded in our drums for respectability. So now it's just words.

I can't live inside yesterday's pain, I can't live without it.

I was thirteen or fourteen before I was thrust into the white world. . . .
I was part of a generation of black children who were raised like
integration soldiers, who were groomed to invade white America. I
don't know how conscious it was, but with my parents it was definitely: "They think you're less than; you've got to be better than."

Stevie Wonder

Born 1944 ◆ singer-songwriter, musician, and social activist
◆ winner of twenty-two Grammy Awards ◆ songs include "I Just
Called to Say I Love You," "For Once in My Life," and
"You Are the Sunshine of My Life"

We all have ability. The difference is how we use it.

You can't base your life on other people's expectations.

Ability may get you to the top, but it takes character to keep you
there.

Mama was my greatest teacher, a teacher of compassion, love and
fearlessness. If love is sweet as a flower, then my mother is that sweet
flower of love.

Just because a man lacks the use of his eyes doesn't mean he lacks
vision.

You gots to work with what you gots to work with.

Carter Godwin Woodson

1875–1950 ◆ "Father of Negro History" ◆ writer, historian, and
journalist ◆ pioneer in the field of black history studies who
founded the Association for the Study of African American Life and
History ◆ books include *The Mis-Education of the Negro* and
The Education of the Negro

When you control a man's thinking you do not have to worry about
his actions. You do not have to tell him not to stand here or go
yonder. He will find his "proper place" and will stay in it. You do not
need to send him to the back door. He will go without being told.
In fact, if there is no back door, he will cut one for his special
benefit.

We need to attain economic independence. You may talk about
rights and all that sort of thing. The people who own this country
will rule this country.

The mere imparting of information is not education. Above all
things, the effort must result in making a man think and do for
himself.

Black people have been mis-educated into confusing their interests
with those of the dominant society.

Liberty is to come to the Negro, not as a bequest, but as a conquest.

Truth could move multitudes with untutored language.

Richard Wright

1908–1960 ◆ poet, writer, playwright, and social activist ◆ books
include *Uncle Tom's Children, Native Son,* and *Eight Men,* and his
autobiographies, *Black Boy* and *American Hunger*

What could I dream of that had the barest possibility of coming
true? I could think of nothing. And, slowly, it was upon exactly that
nothingness that my mind began to dwell, that constant sense of
wanting without having, of being hated without reason.

Men simply copied the realities of their hearts when they built
prisons.

[*on Lead Belly*] Down south the white landlords called him a "bad nigger" and they were afraid of his fists, his bitter biting songs, his twelve-stringed guitar, and his inability to take injustice and like it.

Don't leave inferences to be drawn when evidence can be presented.

White people were not really people; they were a sort of great natural force, like a stormy sky looming overhead or like a deep swirling river stretching suddenly at one's feet in the dark.

Negro folklore contains, in a measure that puts to shame more deliberate forms of Negro expression, the collective sense of Negro life in America. . . . Here are those vital beginnings of a recognition of value in life as it is *lived*.

[A] Negro writer must create in his readers' minds a relationship between a Negro woman hoeing cotton in the South and the men who loll in swivel chairs in Wall Street and take the fruits of her toil.

Men can starve from a lack of self-realization as much as they can from a lack of bread.

In a folklore moulded out of rigorous and inhuman conditions of life . . . the Negro achieved his most indigenous and complete expression. Blues, spirituals, and folk tales recounted from mouth to mouth . . . all these formed the channels through which the racial wisdom flowed.

The artist must bow to the monster of his own imagination.

Each day when you see us black folk upon the dusty land of your farms or upon the hard pavement of your city streets, you usually take it for granted and think you know us, but our history is far stranger than you suspect, and we are not what we seem.

Malcolm X

1925–1965 ◆ a.k.a. Malcolm Little ◆ leader of the Black Power
movement of the sixties and an advocate of Pan-Africanism
◆ minister of the Nation of Islam, which he helped build into a
significant force for the good in black urban communities
◆ *The Autobiography of Malcolm X*

We didn't land on Plymouth Rock, my brothers and sisters— Plymouth Rock landed on us!

Early in life I had learned that if you want something, you had better make some noise.

I come here to make a speech, to tell you the truth. If the truth is anti-American, then blame the truth, don't blame me.

Education is our passport to the future, for tomorrow belongs to the people who prepare for it today.

I am not against violence in self-defense. I don't even call it violence when it's self-defense. I call it intelligence.

Power in defense of freedom is greater than power on behalf of tyranny.

I am neither a fanatic nor a dreamer. I am a black man who loves peace and justice and loves his people.

We must recapture our heritage and our ideals if we are to liberate ourselves from the bonds of white supremacy. We must launch a cultural revolution to unbrainwash an entire people.

You wouldn't be in this country if some enemy hadn't kidnapped you and brought you here. On the other hand, some of you think you came here on the Mayflower.

When a person is a drug addict, he's not the criminal; he's a victim of the criminal. The criminal is the man who brings drugs into the country.

Our family was so poor we would eat the hole out of a doughnut.

In the ghettoes the white man has built for us, he has forced us not to aspire to greater things, but to view life as survival.

The black man's history—when you refer to him as the black man you go way back, but when you refer to him as a Negro, you can only go as far back as the Negro goes. And when you go beyond the shores of America, you can't find a Negro.

The Muslim's X symbolized the true African family name that he could never know. For me, my X replaced the white slavemaster name of "Little" which some blue-eyed devil named Little had imposed upon my paternal forebears.

America's greatest crime against the black man was not slavery or lynchings, but that he was taught to wear a mask of self-hate and self-doubt.

Give your brain as much attention as you do your hair and you'll be a thousand times better off.

Once our freedom struggle is lifted from the confining civil rights label to the level of human rights, our struggle then becomes internationalized.

You cannot separate peace from freedom because no one can be at peace until he has his freedom.

My father was a militant follower of Marcus Garvey's "Back to Africa" movement. The Lansing, Michigan, equivalent of the Ku Klux Klan warned him to stop preaching Garvey's message, but he kept on, and one of my earliest memories is of being snatched awake one night with a lot of screaming going on because our home was afire.

The media's the most powerful entity on earth. . . . They have the power to make the innocent guilty and to make the guilty innocent, and that's power. Because they control the minds of the masses.

If Christianity had asserted itself in Germany, six million Jews would have lived.

When I say the white man is a devil, I speak with the authority of history.

Speaking like this doesn't mean that we're anti-white, but it does mean we're anti-exploitation, we're anti-degradation, we're anti-oppression.

A man who tosses worms in the river isn't necessarily a friend to the fish.

I lay awake amid sleeping Muslim brothers and I learned that pilgrims from every land—every color and class and rank—all snored in the same language.

You're not supposed to be so blind with patriotism that you can't face reality. Wrong is wrong no matter who does it or says it.

We have never initiated any violence against anyone, but we do believe that when violence is practiced against us we should be able to defend ourselves. We do not believe in turning the other cheek.

If it costs me my life in the morning I will tell you tonight that the time has come for the black man to die fighting.

I'm for truth, no matter who tells it.

Frank Yerby

1916–1991 ◆ poet, writer, and playwright ◆ best known for his popular genre fiction — romance and historical novels — several of which were made into movies ◆ expatriate who resided in Spain to avoid racial discrimination in the U.S.

To dreamers Truth is an unlovely thing.

There are two places on earth where human equality is absolute: in the grave and in a prison cell.

Have you ever seen virtue rewarded — in any considerable way I mean — or evil punished? What's punished in life is stupidity and weakness; and morality is an irrelevancy to your hypothetical gods.

Greatness has nothing to do with goodness.

Truth is healing.

What on earth are [African Americans] going to write about when the biological accident of a man's color has been reduced to the total unimportance it ought to have in the scheme of things?

The novelist hasn't any right to inflict on the public his private ideas on politics, religion, or race. If he wants to preach he should go on the pulpit.

I'm not exposed to the kind of life that would enable me to produce a good social protest novel yet . . . I've been spared most of the hard sides of race relations in America.

[on living as an expatriate] My own feeling about this is that I love my country. Unfortunately, my country doesn't love me enough to let me live in it.

Andrew Young

Born 1932 ◆ politician, diplomat, pastor, writer, and mentor to children ◆ mayor of Atlanta ◆ the first African American to serve as the U.S. ambassador to the UN ◆ books include *An Easy Burden: The Civil Rights Movement and the Transformation of America* and *Walk in My Shoes*

It is a blessing to die for a cause, because you can so easily die for nothing.

What people want in the world is not ideology, they want goods and services.

If you're a preacher, you talk for a living, so even if you don't make sense, you learn to make nonsense eloquently.

I'm always suspicious of people who say, "I'm not racist." I feel on much better ground with people who say, "I'm working on overcoming my racism." We've got to approach this problem with as much humility and generosity as we possibly can.

There can be no democracy without truth. There can be no truth without controversy, and there can be no change without freedom.

Politics doesn't control the world, money does.

Whitney Young, Jr.

1921–1971 ◆ civil rights leader, writer, social worker, and fundraiser ◆ worked to end employment discrimination in the U.S ◆ executive director of the National Urban League ◆ books include *To be Equal* and *Beyond Racism: Building an Open Society*

You can holler, protest, march, picket, demonstrate, but somebody must be able to sit in on the strategy conference and plot a course.

It's better to be prepared for an opportunity and not have one than to have an opportunity and not be prepared.

Our ability to create has outreached our ability to use wisely the products of our invention.

[on working within the system] I think to myself, should I get off this train and stand on 125th Street cussing out Whitey to show I am tough? Or should I go downtown and talk to an executive of General Motors about 2,000 jobs for unemployed Negroes.

Liberalism seems to be related to the distance people are from the problem.

The hardest work in the world is being out of work.